アメリカ研究シリーズ No.1

英語で知るアメリカ

8つのテーマで超大国の実情に迫る

杉田米行 編

大学教育出版

はじめに

　本書の最大の特徴は，「二兎を追う」ことです．アメリカに関する教養を高めながら，英語力の向上にも役立つような内容重視の英語テキストです．大学の教養教育等で英語を学んだり一般社会人の方が再度英語に取り組んだりする際に使って欲しいテキストです．執筆者はアメリカ研究の各専門分野において最先端でご活躍しておられ，卓越した研究業績をお持ちの専門家です．なお，本書の企画・刊行にあたっては，アメリカ大使館文化交流部から助成金をいただきました．感謝申し上げます．また，本書の出版の機会を与えてくださいました（株）大学教育出版の佐藤守社長およびいつも的確な編集作業をして下さる編集部安田愛様に御礼申し上げます．また，PTAの役員業務・家事・子育て・介護等を一切引き受けてくれた妻・昌子がいてくれたからこそ，本書を仕上げることができました．いつもありがとうございます．

平成25年9月吉日

杉田米行

英語で知るアメリカ
──8つのテーマで超大国の実情に迫る──

目 次

はじめに ……………………………………………… 杉田米行 ……… *1*

第1章 アメリカのビジネス最前線 ……………… 藤村敬次 ……… *9*

はじめに　*9*
1. アメリカンビジネスの企業規模　*9*
Business USA　*11*
　1. Warm Up　*11*
　2. About Us　*11*
　3. Role Playing "Start a Business"　*14*
　4. Business Licenses and Permits　*16*
　5. Build Your Business Plan　*20*
　6. Articles Recommended for You　*21*
　7. Find Business Counselors That Work Within Your Area　*22*
　8. Success Stories　*22*
　9. Discussion & Giving a feedback　*26*

第2章 アメリカのメディア ……………………… 立花顕一郎 ……… *31*

はじめに　*31*
1. news search（ニュース検索）の一般化　*31*
2. news consumers（ニュース消費者）の台頭　*34*
3. print advertising（紙面広告）の不振　*36*
4. online advertising（オンライン広告）の難しさ　*38*
5. Paywall（有料購読システム）導入の拡大　*42*
6. news app（ニュース閲覧専用アプリ）でより多くの購読者囲い込みを図る大手メディア　*46*
7. 新聞の未来　*48*

第3章　アメリカの憲法と社会 ……………………… 秋葉丈志 ……… 50

はじめに　50
1. The U.S. Constitution: The Most Important Promise　50
2. Equality: Race in U.S. Society　54
3. Privacy: Personal Matters or Not?　58
4. Liberty: Limiting Government Power　61
5. Conclusion: Constitutional Democracy in the U.S.　66

第4章　アメリカ移民の現状 —— ヒスパニック系を事例に ——
……………………… 山元里美 ……… 70

はじめに　70
1. Foreign-born Populations in the United States – 2010　70
2. Analysis of General Hispanic Responses in the U.S. Census 2000　76
3. Demography of Hispanic Identity　82
4. Deportation Relief for Unauthorized Immigrants Youth　86

第5章　アメリカ大統領制と大統領のレトリック
……………………… 西川秀和 ……… 93

はじめに　93
1. 大統領制の起源と建国初期　93
2. ジェファソン・デモクラシー期から南北戦争　95
3. 南北戦争から革新主義の時代　98
4. 革新主義の時代からニュー・ディールまで　102
5. 冷戦と現代　106

第6章 オバマ政権と現代アメリカ
―― オバマ演説に見る光と影 ―― .... 河内信幸 *113*

はじめに　*113*
1. 21世紀のアメリカとオバマの登場　*114*
2. 2008年大統領選挙とオバマ政権の発足　*117*
3. 第1期オバマ政権の実績　*126*
4. オバマ再選への道　*132*

おわりに　*138*

第7章 アメリカの世界観 ―― 国家安全保障戦略（NSS）を読む ――
.... 大賀　哲 *141*

はじめに　*141*
1. George H. W. Bush, *National Security Strategy of the United States*, (August 1, 1991)　*142*
2. Bill Clinton, *A National Security Strategy of Engagement and Enlargement*, (July 1, 1994)　*144*
3. Bill Clinton, *A National Security Strategy for a Global Age*, (December 1, 2000).　*148*
4. George W. Bush, *The National Security Strategy of the United States*, (September 17, 2002).　*151*
5. Barack Obama, *National Security Strategy*, (May 27, 2010).　*156*

おわりに　*160*

第8章 日米の文化学術交流
―― 太平洋の架け橋を志した新渡戸稲造 ――

.... 谷口真紀 …… *162*

はじめに　*162*
1. アメリカとの出会い　*162*
2. アメリカでの『武士道』出版　*166*
3. 日米交換教授としての働き　*169*
4. 満州事変後の渡米　*172*
5. 日米の相互理解の架け橋　*178*

第1章

アメリカのビジネス最前線

はじめに

　Apple，Google，Amazon等，アメリカンドリームの象徴とも言える世界的企業を生み出したアメリカのビジネスの背景には，それを支えるサポート体制がある．昨今ではインターネットの普及と共にその様相も様変わりしてきた．本章では，強いアメリカを生み出す原動力であるアメリカンビジネスのうち，創業間もない企業（startup）と小企業（small business）に対する，国をあげたインターネットによる支援体制（Business USA, Small Business Administration等）について検討する．

1．アメリカンビジネスの企業規模

　アメリカンビジネスというと，一見，巨大企業を思い浮かべがちだが，実はその多くが，日本同様，中小企業で成り立っている．数で日本の4倍とも5倍ともいわれるアメリカ企業の中で中小企業が占める割合について検討する．

1. 次のグラフを見て下の問に答えなさい．

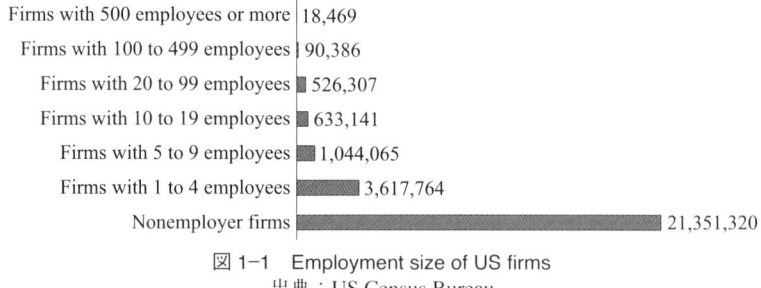

図 1-1　Employment size of US firms
出典：US Census Bureau

(1) ペアを組み，下記の問いを互いに口頭で質問をし，完全な文を用いて答え合いなさい．

1. What is this graph about?

2. What does horizontal axis show?

3. What does vertical axis show?

4. How many companies hire 500 employees or more?

5. Roughly how many companies hire 4 employees or less?

6. Compare answers in question 4 and 5 and draw a conclusion of what size of the business is common in the US.

(2) 1～6の答えを繋ぎあわせ，プレゼンテーションを行うつもりで，上記グラフについて1分程度で説明をしなさい．

Business USA

アメリカでは，インターネットを駆使した起業家支援が盛んである．ここでは，連邦政府の複数機関が作るビジネス支援サイト，BusinessUSAについて検討する．

1. Warm Up
次のポータルサイト (http://business.usa.gov/) にアクセスし，トップページを見た後，ペアを組んで質問し合い，英語で答えなさい．

 1) What kind of portal site is this?
 2) Where do you think are clickable?
 3) What will Americans do using this website?

2. About Us
About Usとは，ホームページ上でサイト運営者について記してあるページのことである．ここでは，Business USAのAbout Usを確認し，サイト運営者について理解を深めていく．

（1）ボキャブラリーチェック
以下の単語 (1-10) とその意味 (a-j) をマッチングしなさい．

1) burdensome	( )	a) 関連した
2) federal bureaucracy	( )	b) 開発中の仕様
3) implement	( )	c) 網羅する
4) relevant to	( )	d) 重荷となる
5) regardless of	( )	e) 連邦政府の官僚組織
6) encompass	( )	f) 貴方独自の条件
7) beta version	( )	g) 競争力
8) on your own terms	( )	h) 〜を備えた
9) competitiveness	( )	i) 実行する
10) be equipped with	( )	j) 〜に関わらず

(2) スキャニング

下記の文章は，上述のウェブサイトにある「About Us」(サイト運営者紹介)である．質問に応じてスキミング（斜め読み）・スキャニング（必要な情報を取り出す）をしなさい．

Too often, interactions with the government are burdensome and frustrating. From seeking out financing opportunities to learning about the latest regulations affecting them, hard-working businesses are spending too much time navigating the federal bureaucracy.

On October 28, 2011, the President issued a challenge to government agencies to think beyond their organizational boundaries in the best interest of serving America's business community, and start thinking and acting more like the businesses they serve. He directed the creation of BusinessUSA, a centralized, onestop platform to make it easier than ever for businesses to access services to help them grow and hire.

BusinessUSA implements a "no wrong door" approach for small businesses and exporters by using technology to quickly connect businesses to the services and information relevant to them, regardless of where the information is located or which agency's website, call center, or office they go to for help. Looking forward, the more federal agencies continue to add resources to BusinessUSA to encompass the full range of business programs and services, the more we will be able to reduce the confusing array of websites that exist today. To ensure that it is oriented towards the needs of the customer, BusinessUSA will be designed, tested, and built with the active feedback of U.S. businesses. This is where you come in.

The beta version of the Business.USA.gov web site is just the first step. In coming weeks and months, guided by your feedback, we will be adding new features and content, and opening new channels of communication to the BusinessUSA network such as call centers, email and social media. We will also seek to integrate state and local governments, as well as related private sector partners. This will help us better deliver z the information you need on your own terms.

To strengthen America's competitiveness in the global economy, businesses will need to be equipped with the best tools and information available to support innovation and job growth in the 21st century. BusinessUSA is your front door to all the government has to offer. Help us make sure it continues to evolve and grow to meet your needs. Sign up for email alerts so you can be the first to find out about changes to BusinessUSA, and use feedback features on the website to let us know what you think. BusinessUSA is designed by businesses, for businesses. Take ownership today.

問：上記の文章について，次の質問に１〜２文の英語で答えなさい．

1) What problem is Business USA meant to solve?

2) Who requested to make Business USA and how did this person request to government agencies?

3) How do they try to improve their website?

4) What do businesses need to have to make American economy more powerful in the world?

3. Role Playing "Start a Business"

Business USA は，新たに起業したい市民に one-stop service を提供する目的で作られており，起業経験のない人でも起業ができるよう，さまざまなサービスが備わっている．ここでは，実際のウェブサイトを参照にしながら，疑似起業家体験を行っていく．

（1）アメリカで起業をするつもりで，Business USA を使ってみよう．
1) Business USA のトップページで Start a Business をクリックする．
ウェブページ http://business.usa.gov/

2) 次のページで get started をクリックし，"Industry & Type"を選び，Do you plan on selling products or services online? のみを選び，Next をクリックする．
☐ Did you invent something?
☑ Do you plan on selling products or services online?
☐ Is your business a franchise?
What business area are you interested in? Select all that apply.
☐ Auto Dealership   ☐ Barber Shop
☐ Beauty Salon   ☐ Child Care Services
☐ Construction Contractor ☐ Debt Collection Agency
☐ Electrician   ☐ Massage Therapist
☐ Plumber   ☐ Restaurant
☐ Other

3) 次のページ，"Location & Operation"でIs your business based in United States?を選び，Zip Code 10010 を入れ，Nextをクリックする．
   ☐ Will your business be based in your home?
   ☐ Will you do business in multiple states or across state lines?
   ☑ Is your business based in United States?
   Zip code where your primary operations are based in ___10010___.

4) 次ページ，"Planning"で"Are you planning on hiring employees?"をクリック．
   ☑ Are you planning on hiring employees?
   ☐ Are you buying an existing business?

5) Resultを見て，それぞれをクリックする．
   ①Business Licenses and Permits　⇒ 本章4へ
   ②Build Your Business Plan　⇒ 本章5へ
   ③Articles Recommended for You　⇒ 本章6へ
   ④Find Business Counselors That Work Within Your Area
   　　　　　　　　　　　⇒ 本章7へ

4. Business Licenses and Permits

(1) ボキャブラリーチェック

文中に登場する単語 1) 〜 15) と (a) 〜 (o) をマッチングしなさい．

1) comply with ( )	(a) 源泉徴収税
2) wide range of ( )	(b) 看板
3) obtain ( )	(c) 控除する
4) identification (ID) ( )	(d) 許可証
5) tax withholding ( )	(e) 労災保険
6) permit ( )	(f) 職業上の
7) occupational ( )	(g) を遵守する
8) proprietorship ( )	(h) 屋号
9) trade name ( )	(i) 広範囲の
10) Workers Compensation Insurance ( )	(j) 身分証明書
11) deduct ( )	(k) 民間業者
12) commercial carrier ( )	(l) 個人事業者
13) jurisdiction ( )	(m) 土地利用
14) signage ( )	(n) 管轄
15) zoning ( )	(o) 取得する

アメリカでは，連邦（Federal），州（State），と市や郡（local）で行政枠が分かれており，ビジネスを始める際，業種やビジネスの内容により，行政単位ごとに登記や認可が必要となる．ここでは，それらの概要について検討する．

(2) スキャニング&スピーキング

次の文は上記①Business Licenses and Permits の中にある情報である．本文にさっと目を通した後，下記の質問の答えを文中より抜いてメモを取り，ペアを組んで質問しあいなさい．

In order to start and operate your business, one must comply with a wide range of local, state and federal rules.

第1章　アメリカのビジネス最前線　17

Federal Licenses and Permits
Employer Identification Number (EIN)
Employers with employees, business partnerships, and corporations, must obtain an Employer Identification Number (EIN) from the U.S. Internal Revenue Service. The EIN is also known as an Employer Tax ID and Form SS-4.
U.S. Internal Revenue Service Phone: 1-800-829-4933
- Guide to Employer Identification Number
- Apply Online

State Licenses and Permits
New York Tax Registration
Businesses that operate within NY are required to register for one or more tax-specific identification numbers, licenses or permits, including income tax withholding, sales and use tax (sellers permit), and unemployment insurance tax. Contact the following agency for more information about business registration and your tax obligations:
- General Tax Information and Forms

Business Licenses
Information about how to obtain business and occupational licenses and permits
- Online Permit Assistance and Licensing
- Professional and Occupational Licenses

Report New Hires
All employers are required to report newly and rehired employees to their states Directory of New Hires within 20 days of their hire or re-hire data.

Business Entity Registration - Forms and Applications
If your business is a corporation, a non-profit, a limited liability company or a

partnership (limited, or limited liability) you must register with the following state agency.

If your business is a sole proprietorship, you do not need to register your business with the state. However, many states require a sole proprietor to use their own name for the business name unless they formally file another name as a trade name, or fictitious name.

Disability Insurance
Obtain Disability Insurance
Temporary disability insurance provides benefit payments to insured workers for time off work due to a non-work related illness or injury. Employers are responsible for deducting disability insurance tax from employees' wages and reporting these taxes to the state.

Workers Compensation Insurance
Find Workers Comp Requirements
Businesses with employees are required to carry Workers Compensation Insurance coverage through a commercial carrier, on a self-insured basis, or through the state Workers Compensation Insurance program.

Unemployment Insurance
Get Unemployment Tax Requirements
Businesses with employees are required to pay unemployment insurance taxes under certain conditions. If your business is required to pay these taxes, you must register your business with your states workforce agency:

Local Permits
You may be required to apply for permits and licenses from your local government (e.g., city or county). Every place has different requirements. The

following are common types of local permits and licenses.
- Business Licenses / Tax Permits - from your city or county clerk or revenue department. Many jurisdictions require a trader's license or tax certificate in order to operate.
- Building Permit - from your city or county building and planning department. This permit is generally required if you are constructing or modifying your place of business.
- Health Permit - from your city or county health department.
- Occupational Permit - from your city or county building and planning development department. This permit is required for home-based business in some jurisdictions.
- Signage Permit - from your city or county building and planning department. Some jurisdictions require a permit before you can erect a sign for your business.
- Alarm Permit - from you city or county police or fire department. If you have installed a burglar or fire alarm, you will likely need an alarm permit.
- Zoning Permit - from your city or county building and planning department. This permit is generally required if you are developing land for specific commercial use.
- Depending on the nature of your business, you may need other types of licenses specific to your business. Check with the following local government(s) for more.

問

1) If you would like to start a business in the US, what do you need to comply with?

2) What is EIN? Who issues it to business owners?

3) If you are a business with employees, what do you need to do in the State of New York? List at least 7 items and discuss with your partner.

4) What is disability insurance and what does employer have to do about the insurance? Explain.

5) Explain ①zoning permit and ②occupational permit.

5. Build Your Business Plan

（1）ボキャブラリーチェック

下記の1)〜8) と (a)〜(h) をとマッチングしなさい．

1) roadmap ( )		(a) 収益を増やす
2) grow revenue ( )		(b) 特定する
3) identify ( )		(c) 潜在顧客
4) competitors ( )		(d) 行程
5) legal requirement ( )		(e) 法的要件
6) potential customer ( )		(f)（金銭の）貸し手
7) projection ( )		(g) 計画・予測
8) lender ( )		(h) 競合

（2）リスニング＆スピーキング

次のウェブサイトで15ページの②Build Your Business Planに関する説明を何度が聞いたのち，以下の質問についてメモを取りなさい．メモがとれたら，ペアを組んで一方が質問，一方が答えなさい．終わったら，役割を変えて同じことを繰り返しなさい．

How to write a business plan on You Tube.

http://youtu.be/SMr_uLZV-eM

（字幕機能がついているが，少なくとも2，3度は字幕なしで聞くこと）

1) How does a business plan help you succeed?

2) What are six steps to create a business plan? Please fill in the blank.

1. _____	2. Company Overview
3. _____	4. Products and Services
5. _____	6. _____

3) What is executive summary? Explain.

4) What is the difference between "marketing research" and "marketing and sales"?

5) Why is financial projection important?

6. Articles Recommended for You

下記 1)〜8) は，**Articles recommended for you** の **Article List** である．タイトルを見て，どのような情報が得られそうか想定し，(a)〜(h) とマッチングをしなさい．

1) Online Business Law	( )
2) Online Businesses	( )
3) Employment and Labor Law	( )
4) Find Business Loans, Grants & Other Financial Assistance	( )
5) What State Licenses and Permits Does Your Business Need?	( )
6) How to Name a Business	( )
7) 20 Questions Before Starting a Business	( )
8) Follow These 10 Steps to Starting a Business	( )

The article is:

(a) like a check-list for a new business owner.
(b) for how to search fund sources for business startups.
(c) about regulations relevant to selling products on the Internet.
(d) for understanding hiring rules provided by the governments.
(e) to help you decide your trade name.
(f) a procedure for a new business owner.
(g) general guidelines and tips for selling products on the Internet.
(h) to find authorization required.

7. Find Business Counselors That Work Within Your Area

次の文は **3 Role Playing "Start a Business"** の result ④ **Find Business Counselors That Work Within Your Area** からの一部抜粋である．下記の文をさっと見た後，下記の質問に答えなさい．

Small Business Development Centers [?] Baruch College SBDC *(0 miles away)* 55 Lexington Avenue Field Center, Room 2-140 New York, NY View All	SCORE Chapters [?] New York City SCORE *(2 miles away)* 26 Federal Plaza Room 3100 New York, NY View All

(1) What do you think this list is?
(2) What kind of help do you think business owners will get?
(3) Based on what do they list their offices?

8. Success Stories

Business USA への参加政府機関のうち，Small Business Association (SBA) は，Startup や Small Business を支援する機関として有名である．SBA を通じて成功を収めている企業は Business USA および SBA のウェブサイトを通じて紹介されている．2つの成功事例を紹介する．

The Fresh Diet

(1) ボキャブラリーチェック：下記1)〜5) と (a)〜(e) をマッチングしなさい．

1) finance	( )	(a) 担保
2) revenue	( )	(b) 頭金
3) mortgage	( )	(c) 資金を調達する
4) down payment	( )	(d) 年代順に
5) chronologically	( )	(e) 収益

(2) リーディング＆スピーキング

次の文を2分程度で読み，下記の質問ごとに，ペアを組んで互いに口頭で内容説明をする練習をしなさい．

When Zalmi Duchman started The Fresh Diet in 2005, the company was financed on credit cards, Zalmi's wife was doing the cooking from their home, and Zalmi was delivering the food after work.

After Yosef Schwartz, a Le Cordon Bleu trained chef, moved to Florida to become his partner, the company quickly outgrew Zalmi's kitchen. By 2007, they had grown from 13 to 100 clients, with revenues of more than $1 million and 7 employees.

The Fresh Diet delivers three freshly prepared meals and two snacks directly to customer's doors each day. The menu supports healthy weight loss through calorie control and proper nutritional balance.

In mid-2007, Zalmi decided to buy a similar company with small

写真1-2

operations in Florida, New York and Chicago. Zalmi mortgaged his condo for the $200,000 down payment and obtained an SBA backed loan for $900,000 to purchase the company. By 2008 revenues reached $5 million.

In 2009, Zalmi used a second SBA backed loan for $225,000 to acquire a second company and take over all their own cooking operations. The Fresh Diet is projecting revenues of $30 million for 2011 and currently employs over 200 people nationwide and over 100 drivers.

設問：
1) Who founded this company and who is his/her partner?
2) What is their business and what do you think is their selling point?
3) How did their business grow? Explain chronologically from the start to 2011.
4) What kind of governmental support did they get?

Delivering Success: Entrepreneurial Spirit

(1) リスニング＆ライティング

下記のウェブページにアクセスし，写真のWarren Brown氏のインタビューを聞いた後，設問に答えなさい．

> ホームページアドレスを入力 http://youtu.be/5t3eELBpKoM
> または，YouTubeの検索ボックスにて，SBA Delivering Success: Entrepreneurial Spirit と入力して該当動画を探す．

注）字幕機能がついているが，2〜3度聞いてもわからなければ使用すること．

1) What business does he own?

2) What is his background?

3) What didn't he like about his former job?

4) What drove him to start his current job?

5) How did SBA support his business?

6) What do business owners need to do?

(2) サマリー&スピーキング

下記に記した手順で，サマリー（要約）とスピーキングを行いなさい．

手順1　(1) の答えを，下の例を参照に，会話調になるよう編集し，下記に書き出しなさい．（下記の例を丸写ししないこと）

手順2　上のサマリーをペアで交換し，文法・語彙等確認し合いなさい．

手順3　ペアにて，原稿をみながら，リズミカルにしゃべる練習をしなさい．

手順4　原文通りでなくとも良いので，上記の原稿を見ないで，リズミカルにしゃべる練習をしなさい．

Summary Example：

Warren owns a bakery and café. When he was younger, his interest was completely different. He studied American history in college and studied Public Health and Law in law school and became a lawyer at a governmental institution. The job was really good but he couldn't feel passionate about the job because it was all about black and white on paper or supporting and not supporting an argument. So he simply followed his heart and started a business. At the beginning, he needed to get capital to bake and operate his business so he loaned money from a local community bank. SBA didn't loan him money but backed him up for his loaning. He says that business owners have to be prepared for the worst scenario and also, at the same time, they have to be cheerleaders for everybody. He also mentioned that business owners have to balance between realistic part, like achieving sales target and knowing the product, and bright future of their business

特徴：
1. なるだけ難しい単語はさけ，基本単語でまとめるのが望ましい．
2. 日本語と異なり，**He**,,,**He** と同じ主語を連続で続けても違和感はない．
3. 事実は正確にとらえるべきだが，多少の主観が入った「脚色」「表現のずれ」は大きな問題とはしない．

9. Discussion & Giving a feedback

(1) ディスカッション

1) What do you think is important to get success in Business?

2) Why do you think governmental help like Business USA or SBA is helpful for startup businesses?

(2) フィードバック

Business USA に自分でアクセスし，ブラウズした感想を 200 語〜 300 語で書きなさい．書く際に下記の問いに答えること．

Business USA ウェブサイトアドレス：http://business.usa.gov/

1) What were the good points about the website?

2) What were the points that need to be improved?

解答
アメリカンビジネスの企業規模
(1) 解答例（口頭ベース）
1. This graph is about the employment size of US firms.
2. Horizontal axis shows the number of firms.
3. Vertical axis shows the firm size based on the number of employees.
4. 18,469 firms hire 500 employees or more.
5. Roughly 25 million firms hire 4 employees or less.

6. This means that small business is more common type of business than other sizes of businesses.

(2) 解答例（口頭ベース）

This graph shows the employment size of US firms. Horizontal Axis shows the number of firms, and vertical axis shows the firm size based on the number of employees. Compared to 18,469 firms with 500 employees or more, roughly 25 million firms are with 4 employees or less. This indicates that, just like Japan's case, the majority of US business consists of small to mid-size businesses.

BusinessUSA

1. Warm up

解答例

1) It is called Business USA and this site helps business owners in U.S.
2) Square banners in the middle, Tour, Resources, About Us, Contact Us on the upper right.
3) They try to search how to start a business, get disaster assistance, access financing and so on.

2. About Us

(1) ボキャブラリーチェック

1) d 2) e 3) i 4) a 5) j 6) c 7) b 8) f 9) g 10) h

(2) 解答例

1) It is meant to solve burdensome and frustrating interactions with the government agencies.
2) President challenged and requested them to think beyond their organizational boundaries and ask them to create a centralized, one-stop service to help business communities.
3) More programs and services will be added over time, and the website is improved with the active feedback of U.S. businesses.
4) Businesses need to be equipped with the best tool and information available to support innovation and job growth in the 21st century.

3. Role Play "Start a Business"

設問なし

4. Business Licenses and Permits

(1) ボキャブラリーチェック

1) g 2) i 3) o 4) d 5) a 6) d 7) f 8) l 9) h 10) e 11) c 12) k 13) n 14) b 15) m

(2) スキャニング&スピーキング　解答例

1) a wide range of local, states and federal rules.

2) Employer Identification Number and it is issued by Internal Revenue Services.

3) Tax registration, business licenses, report new hires, business entity registration, obtain disability insurance, Workers' Compensation Insurance and Unemployment Insurance.

4) Disability insurance provides benefit payments to insured workers for time off work due to a non-work related illness or injury. Employers need to deduct it from employees wages and report them to the state.

5) Permit may be required to put up a sign of your business. Zoning Permit is required when developing land for commercial use. Occupational Permit is needed when you have home-based business, in some cases.

5. Build Your Business Plan

(1) ボキャブラリーチェック　1) d 2) a 3) b 4) h 5) e 6) c 7) g 8) f

(2) リスニング&スピーキング

1) It sets the direction for early years of business.

2) 1. Executive Summary 3. Market Research 5 Marketing and Sales 6 Financial Projection

3) Executive summary explains your business and identify your customer. Business owners need to make a strong case of how you make your business successful.

4) Marketing research discusses how well you understand the market and competitors and it should also include legal requirements. Marketing and sales should discuss how you will identify potential customers and how you want to sell your products-online or offline sales, etc.

5) It is important because it shows your investors and lenders how you keep money and positive cash flow.

6. Articles Recommended for You

(1) c (2) g (3) d (4) b (5) h (6) e (7) a (8) f

7. Find Business Counselors That Work Within Your Area

1. This is a list for business counselors.

2. They can get help how to do their business.
3. Based on the distance from their location.

8. Success Stories
The Fresh Diet
(1) ボキャブラリーチェック
1) c 2) e 3) a 4) b 5) d
(2) リーディング&スピーキング
設問（解答例）：
1) Zalmi Duchman (and his wife) founded the company and Yosef Schwartz is his partner.
2) Their business is called The Fresh Diet, and they operate cooking and delivery service of food for healthy weight loss. Their selling point is that the food is delivered to customer's door and it's healthy and nutritional food.
3) At the start, their business was almost like part-time business. Zalmi delivered food after work, and his wife was cooking at her own kitchen. But after Yosef Schwartz joined the company, the business grew very quickly. By 2007, they grew from 13 to 100 clients and 1 million dollars in sales. By 2008, the revenue reached 5 million. In 2011, their company is projecting 30 million dollars in sales and is employing more than 200 people.
4) SBA backed their loan for 900,000 dollars and 225,000 dollars for expanding their business.

Delivering Success
(1) リスニング&ライティング
1) Warren owns a bakery and café.
2) He studied American history in college and studied Public Health and Law in law school and became a lawyer at a governmental institution.
3) The job was really good, but he couldn't feel passionate about the job because it was all about black and white on paper or supporting and not supporting an argument.
4) He simply followed his heart.
5) SBA didn't loan him money but backed him up for his loaning.
6) He says that business owners have to be prepared for the worst scenario and also, at the same time, they have to be cheerleaders for everybody. He also mentioned that business owners have to balance between realistic part, like achieving sales target and knowing the product, and bright future of their business.

(2) サマリー&スピーキングテキスト内「Summary Example」参照

9. Discussion & Feedback
1. 自由解答
2. 自由解答

参考文献
Small Business Administration. (n.d.). *Small Business Administration*. Retrieved March 15, 2013, from Delivering Sucess: Entrepreneurial Sprit: http://www.youtube.com/watch?v=5t3eELBpKoM
U.S. Government. (n.d.). *Success Story: The Fresh Diet*. Retrieved April 15, 2013, from BusinessUSA: http://business.usa.gov/success_story/fresh-diet
U.S. Government. (n.d.). *Business USA*. Retrieved March 26, 2013, from http://business.usa.gov/about-us
US Census Bureau. (n.d.). *Statistics about Business Size (including Small Business)*. Retrieved March 15, 2013, from U.S. Census Bureau: http://www.census.gov/econ/smallbus.html

第2章

アメリカのメディア

はじめに

本章ではアメリカのニュース・メディアのうち特に新聞業界が直面しているビジネス環境の大きな変化について，それを端的に表すキーワードを読み解きながら概観する．

1．news search（ニュース検索）の一般化

インターネットを用いて世界中のニュースを閲覧することは今日では当たり前のことになっているが，それが可能になったのはわずか20年前だった．

1993年4月30日にCERN（欧州原子核研究機構）がworld wide webの技術を著作権使用料無料で公開した．この技術はCERNに在籍していたイギリス人物理学者Tim Berners-Lee（ティム・バーナーズ＝リー）が1989年に開発していたが，もしもこの時に無料公開されていなかったらインターネットの利用者拡大は今より大幅に緩やかなペースで進行していたかもしれない．

1990年代半ばになると，Netscape Navigator（ネットスケープ・ナビゲーター）やInternet Explorer（インターネット・エクスプローラー）等のパーソナル・コンピューター用インターネット・ブラウザ・ソフトウェアが登場してきた．

インターネットで情報提供を行う企業や個人が爆発的に増え，PCをインターネットに接続して使うことが一般的になっていった．

このような機会を絶妙に捉えて，情報検索サイトの草分けであるYahoo!（ヤ

フー）が会社法人としてカリフォルニア州で営業を開始したのは1995年であり，その後塵を拝したものの現在では世界一利用されている検索サイトGoogle（グーグル）が設立されたのが1998年である．

　インターネット上の情報量が天文学的に増加するにつれて，欲しい情報を見つけ出すことが困難になりつつあったPCユーザーにとってYahoo!やGoogleはまさに渡りに船だった．オンライン情報検索が容易になったおかげで，知りたい情報やニュースがあればオンラインで検索するようになった．その当時から今に至るまでデスクトップPCユーザーにとってのニュースの入り口が検索サイトであるのは以上のような経緯によるのである．

　しかし，ビジネスを開始したばかりの検索サイトには大きな悩みが一つあった．利用者の数が急激に増加しているにも関わらず，それをどのように収益に結びつけられるのかという疑問に対する答えを知らなかったのである．

　その状況は1920年代にラジオが登場したばかりのアメリカに似ていた．ペンシルバニア州ピッツバーグでウエスチング・ハウス・エレクトリック社が1920年にラジオの実験放送を開始し，2年後に商務省の正式免許を受けている．その直後に競うように開局したラジオ局のほとんどは非営利団体であったという．これらの放送局はどのように利益を上げるかというビジネス・プランも無いままに操業していたのである．

　時代の違いこそあれ，新たなメディアとして登場したラジオ局も検索サイトも収益確保の方策として最終的に目を付けたのは広告であった．後述するように，インターネットを利用するビジネス・モデルはGoogleがkeyword targeting advertising（検索連動型広告）を開始してから急激に成長し始めるのである．

　アメリカのITジャーナリストであるスティーブン・レヴィ（2011）は，グーグルが広告事業に真剣に取り組み始めたのは1999年後半であったと指摘している．それ以後，わずか10年ほどで，Googleはインターネット上に巨大な広告市場を構築してしまうのである．対照的に，TVや新聞などの既存メディアはその間に広告収入の大幅な落ち込みに苦しむこととなったのである．

　既存メディアが失ったのは広告収入だけではない．アメリカの非営利調査機関ピュー・リサーチ・センター（2012）によると，今日ではアメリカの18歳以上

の人口の4分の3以上がデスクトップ・コンピューターかノート・パソコンを所有している．彼らはTVや新聞などを利用する時間を減らす一方で，インターネットを利用する時間を増やしている．その結果，アメリカ人がニュースに接触する手段のうち，地方テレビ局のニュース番組，全国ネットのニュース番組に次いでインターネットは3番目の地位を得ている．新聞やラジオよりも頻繁にニュース・ソースとしてインターネットが選ばれている．

　アメリカにおける情報通信技術の進歩と普及は早い．最近の最も大きな変化はスマートフォン・ユーザーの急増である．Consumer Electronics Association（全米家電協会，略称はCEA）が2013年4月22日に公表した調査結果によると，アメリカ人家庭へのスマートフォン普及率は58％に達した（対前年比12％増）．6,900万世帯がスマートフォンを所有していることになる．しかも，スマートフォンに対する潜在的な需要は依然として高いままである．アメリカの消費者の29％が1年以内にスマートフォンを購入する予定であるとCEAの調査に答えている．

英作文問題

　英作文の問題に挑戦してみよう．下記の日本文を英文に訳しなさい．

問題1. インターネットはニュース検索をとても容易にした．
ヒント．make ～ much easier（～をとても容易にする）を使おう．

問題2. スマートフォン所有率は2013年に50％を超えた．
ヒント．「スマートフォン普及率」はsmartphone ownership，「超える」は動詞exceedが使える．

関連語
search engine　検索エンジン：インターネット上に存在する情報を検索するためのウェブ・サイトやシステム全般のこと．検索専用のウェブ・サイトは特にsearch site（検索サイト）と呼ばれることもある．
portal site　ポータル・サイト：天気予報，ニュース，占いなどさまざまなコンテンツを集めて，ネット・サーフィンの起点として利用できるように構成されているウェブ・サイト．

BYOD　bring your own device：私物の情報端末を持ち込む：個人が所有するモバイル情報端末を職場に持ち込んで使用すること．世界的に見ると，アジア・太平洋地域の国々では職場へのBYOD普及率は高いが，日本は大きく後れを取っている．アメリカの情報誌Wiredの日本語版ウェブ・サイトによると，タイでは93％の企業が個人のノート・パソコン，スマートフォン，タブレットPCを職場で使用することを認めている．中国では95％，台湾では93％，韓国では90％の企業がBYODを導入．対照的に日本での普及率はわずか22％．日本企業はセキュリティを重視し過ぎるあまり，従業員の仕事効率化と新しいワークスタイルの導入を犠牲にしている，とWired誌は指摘している．

2．news consumers（ニュース消費者）の台頭

　急激なモバイル化の大波がアメリカのニュース・メディアに揺さぶりをかけている．スマートフォンなど複数のモバイル情報端末を所有し，インターネットに常時接続して多くのニュースに接触する人々が増えている．彼らはnews consumers（ニュース消費者）と呼ばれ，新聞社，雑誌社，テレビ局，ラジオ局といった既存のメディア産業に対してビジネス・モデルの変更を促すほどの影響力をもつようになってきている．

　このようなmultiple digital devices（多様なデジタル機器）の時代を先導したのは言うまでもなくアメリカのアップル社が2007年6月に発売した初代iPhoneだが，それに対抗してグーグル社が開発した携帯情報端末用プラットフォームのアンドロイド搭載のスマートフォン利用者も増え続けている．

　アメリカのインターネット分析会社コムスコアネットワークが2012年10月から2013年1月にかけて実施した調査によると，アメリカのスマートフォン所有者のうち，37％がiPhoneユーザーで，韓国のサムスン電子社や台湾のHTC社などを含むアンドロイド搭載スマートフォンのユーザーが52％である．加えて，news consumersの中にはiPadなどのtablet PC（タブレット型コンピューター）やnote PC（ノート・パソコン）をも併用している人が多い．

　CEAの調査では，Tablet PCの年間販売増加率はスマートフォンの年間販売増加率を5％上回る17％で，アメリカ人家庭への普及率は39％に達している．

　このようなモバイル機器利用者の特徴を人口統計学的に調べたピュー・リサー

チ・センター（2013）によれば，過半数が男性で（news consumersの59%），学歴が高く（61%が大卒以上の学歴を持つ），比較的若い人で（18歳〜29歳），アメリカの北西部や中西部の人口非密集地に住む人が多いという．

　スマートフォンが初めて登場してから10年に満たないにもかかわらず，news consumersの急速な増加が既存ニュース・メディアにとって大きな脅威となりつつあるのはなぜだろうか．その理由は，彼らが「消費者」と呼ばれているものの，ほとんどの場合はニュースを無料で閲覧しているに過ぎず，情報提供者であるメディアの収入を圧迫し続けているからである．

　既存メディアのほとんどは紙媒体や独占的電波の利用権に依存したビジネス・モデルを長年運営してきたため，日々進歩しているデジタル機器とインターネットを最大限に活用した新しい収益モデルを構想し切れていない．

英作文問題

　英作文の問題に挑戦してみよう．下記の日本文を英文に訳しなさい．

問題3．ますます多くの人がスマートフォンを使い始めている
ヒント．an increasing number of 〜（ますます多くの〜）を使おう．

問題4．Androidユーザーの数はiPhoneユーザーの数を追い越した．
ヒント．動詞はoutnumber（〜に数で勝る）を使うとシンプルな英文になる．

関連語

Internet browsing software　インターネット閲覧ソフト：インターネット上のサイトを閲覧するためのソフトウェアのこと．ウェブ・ブラウザと呼ばれたり，単にブラウザと簡略化されたりすることも多い．

digital maven　デジタルの達人

digital omnivore　デジタル機器全般に貪欲な人：上記2つの言葉は日本語で言うところの「おたく」のように複数のデジタル情報機器にはまって，それらを自由自在に使いこなす人たちを表す．

3. print advertising（紙面広告）の不振

　インターネットに接続するモバイル情報端末の種類と利用者が拡大した結果，私たちがインターネットを用いてニュースに接触する機会は格段に増えている．このようにニュースに対する需要が増えているにもかかわらず，ニュースを配信するメディアの収益が悪化している最大の要因は広告収入の落ち込みである．新聞業界の収入落ち込みの内訳を詳細に見よう．

　アメリカ新聞協会（Newspaper Association of America, 略称NAA）が加盟17新聞社を対象に行った調査によると，2012年の総収入は386億ドルで，前年に比べて9億ドル（2%）の減少だった．収入のうち，最も大きな割合を占めたのは昔ながらの稼ぎ頭であるprint advertising（紙面広告または紙媒体広告）で，189億ドル（総収入の46%に相当），前年比9%減である．

　新聞紙面という限られた情報スペースの希少価値が今よりも高かった時代には，企業の多くが高額な広告料を新聞社に支払っていた．しかし，インターネット上に多種多様な広告を展開できる今日では，企業はメディアミックス戦略を綿密に練り上げてから媒体ごとの広告費配分を決めている．

　新聞社側はprint advertisingのこのような大きな落ち込みを埋め合わせるための新たな収入源を確保できていないので，人員整理をせざるを得ない．ピュー・リサーチ・センターの調査（2013）によれば，2000年から2012年にかけて新聞社では常勤職を30%削減し，1978年以来初めて常勤職員の総数が4万人を割り込んだ．大規模な人員削減を行った結果，新聞社が提供するニュースの質と量への悪影響を懸念する声が強くなっている．

　日刊紙の発行を週7日から週3日に減らしてまで生き残りを図る新聞社さえ出始めている．これはルイジアナ州ニューオリンズ市の地方紙 The Times-Picayune（ザ・タイムズ・ピカユーン）を発行している Advance Publications 社が2012年10月に実施した事業再編策であり，印刷紙の購入代と配送コストを削減することで長期の生き残りを目指す経営努力の一環である．人口約36万人のニューオリンズは今では日刊紙のないアメリカ最大の都市である．

地方紙が苦境に陥っている理由はprint advertisingの種類中でも，特にclassified advertising（案内広告）部門の収益の著しい落ち込みである．classified advertisingの紙面には「売ります」，「買います」，「求人」，「不動産情報」などのカテゴリーごとに短い広告文が多数掲載されている．それらの広告料金は行数で決まることが多い．そのため，安価な広告手法として主に地方都市の中小企業から個人事業者，学生などにいたるまで幅広い利用者が多いのが特徴である．

ピュー・リサーチ・センター（2013）によると，アメリカ全土の新聞社が2012年に計上したclassified advertisingの収入合計は47億ドルだった．この数字は2010年のピーク時（総額196億ドル）に比べると80％以上も少ない．この分野ではインターネットの無料専用サイト利用者が急増しているからである．

日常の暮らしの中で不要になった品物を転売したり，アパートの借家人を求める不動産情報を流したりと，人々の生活に密着しているclassified advertisingは，その即時性や検索の利便性において新聞よりもネットの方がはるかに使い勝手が良い．地方紙が巻き返すのは簡単ではない．

大手新聞社には中小新聞社とは異なる収入減の原因がある．たとえば，ニューヨーク・タイムズの広告収入の不振が続いている原因はnational advertising（全米規模の広告）の減少だ．不動産会社，映画会社，自動車メーカーなどがnational advertisingキャンペーンの予算を縮小しているのが響いている．

英作文問題

英作文の問題に挑戦してみよう．下記の日本文を英文に訳しなさい．

問題5. 紙面掲載広告が新聞業界の総収入の46％を占めた．
ヒント．熟語make up ～ %（～ %を占める）を使うとシンプルな英文になる．

問題6. 案内広告は中小企業にとって大変便利である．
ヒント．中小企業はsmall and midsize companiesである．

関連語
advertising revenue　広告収入
personal advertisement　個人広告，個人による広告

4．online advertising（オンライン広告）の難しさ

　新聞社はインターネット上で個人消費者のニーズに応じた商品やサービスについての広告を臨機応変に配信することが苦手である．そのような広告手法はonline advertising（オンライン広告）と呼ばれ，Googleなどのsearch engine運営企業が得意とする分野であり，高度なbehavioral targeting（行動ターゲティング）技術が必要不可欠である．

　behavioral targetingとはonline advertising に用いられる手法で，個々の消費者がどのようなウェブ・サイトを閲覧し，何の情報を検索し，何を買っているか，どこに住んでいるかなどの情報を逐次集めて分析し，personalized（個人に特化した）広告を検索結果の画面に表示する技術である．

　このような手法を用いることでonline advertisingは消費者の興味や思考を反映する広告をinteractive（双方向的）に配信できるので，広告のcost effectiveness（費用対効果）を高めることができる．代表的な例としては，Googleのkeyword targeting advertising（検索連動型広告）がある．広告主は特定のキーワードとそれに関連する広告文をあらかじめGoogleと契約して登録しておき，そのキーワードと一致または関連する検索が行われれば，登録しておいた広告文が検索結果の画面に表示される．

　online advertisingには他にもさまざまな手法があり，online classified advertisingもその一種だし，banner advertising（バナー広告）やsocial network advertising（ソーシャル・ネットワーク広告）等もある．

　これらの広告分野では競合する企業同士の競争がし烈である．たとえば，業界最大手のGoogleの2013年の業績を見てみると，売上高は同社の創業15年目にして初めて500億円の大台を突破し，501億7,500万ドル（前年比32％増）に達した．この数字は先述のNAA加盟17新聞社の収入合計である386億ドルを

大きく上回っている．

　Googleの売上高のうちonline advertising収入の占める割合は94％だった．17新聞社のonline advertising収入は平均すると売上高のわずか11％（34億ドル）で，Googleとは比べようもない状況である．

　新聞社がonline advertisingを苦手とするもう一つの理由は，若者の消費行動を把握するのが困難であることだ．そもそも今日の若者の多くは紙の新聞を読む習慣がないので，新聞社と彼らの接点が少ない．

　NAAの先述とは別の調査報告によると，アメリカの新聞購読者の平均年齢は54歳で，テレビのイブニング・ニュース視聴者の平均年齢である53歳とほぼ同じである．このような平均年齢の高さの背景にあるのは若者の既存メディア離れとモバイル情報端末への移行である．

　18歳から34歳のアメリカ人に絞ると，実に48％がモバイル機器しか使わないnews consumersである．スマートフォンとタブレットPCのユーザーの平均年齢はそれより多少上がって37歳だが，Twitter（ツイッター）利用者の平均年齢は32歳である．若者にそっぽを向かれたメディアの将来は暗い．

　新聞社が若者を対象とした広告キャンペーンを行うとすれば，mobile advertising（モバイル広告＝モバイル情報端末に広告を配信すること）に力を入れる必要がある．NAAによると，17新聞社の2012年の総収入のうち，mobile advertising収入の占める割合は1％にも満たないが，前年に比べて2倍（100％増）の伸びを見せている．しかし，この分野にも新たに強力なライバルが登場した．FacebookやTwitterが2012年からmobile advertisingを開始したのである．

　ソーシャル・ネットワークによる広告配信は始まったばかりにもかかわらず非常に有望である．アメリカの調査会社eMarketerによると，2012年のアメリカにおけるmobile advertisingは前年比約2.8倍（178％増）の41億1,000万ドルの市場規模となった．

　特に広告市場に参入したばかりのFacebookの躍進はめざましく，mobile display advertising（mobile advertisingの手法の一つで，モバイル情報端末用のウェブ・ページの一部として埋め込まれて表示される広告）の分野で市場占有率第1位（21.1％）を獲得した．第2位のGoogleは17％で，Twitterは第4位

（7.3％）につけた．

　mobile advertisingのさまざまな手法のうち，最大収益を上げているmobile search advertising（モバイル検索広告）では，Googleの強さが圧倒的で，およそ50％の市場占有率を維持している．この分野でもFacebookは善戦していて，3億9,090万ドルのモバイル広告収入を挙げ，9.5％のシェアを獲得した．Twitterの市場占有率も7.3％となっている．

　eMarketerの予測によると，アメリカのmobile adverting市場は2017年までに270億ドルを超える規模にまで拡大し，digital advertising全体の45％近くを占めるようになる見込みである．

　online advertisingの未来は明るいようだが，他方，多くのメディアや広告主はモバイル時代の消費者の扱いにくさに頭を抱えている．アメリカの大手通信社Associated Pressの元記者でIP業界に詳しいRachel Metz（レイチェル・メッツ）は，FacebookやTwitterといったソーシャル・ネットワークの利用者の多くは，one-way message（一方的なメッセージ）に拒否反応を見せるという．彼らはニュースや特定の商品に対する個人的な意見を主体的に発信し，それを友人やフォロワーとシェアすることで消費行動に結びつける傾向が強い．彼らはparticipatory consumers（参加型の消費者）として，製品に対して広告主と対等な発言権を主張するのである．

　online advertisingに対しては，ウェブ・ページ閲覧者のプライバシーを侵害しているという批判も強まっている．実際，Googleは最近，東京地裁から同社の検索予測システムに問題があるとの判決を受けている．

　『毎日新聞』2013年4月15日電子版によると，訴えたのは東京都内の男性で，Googleの検索サイトで自分の名前を入力すると，本人とはまったく関係のない犯罪を連想させる語句が自動的に表示され，名誉を傷つけられたと主張している．裁判で焦点となったのは，単語を入力すると関連語句を自動的に予測表示するGoogleのサジェスト機能であったが，東京地裁はこの男性の表示差し止め請求を認め慰謝料30万円の支払いを命じた．Googleのサジェスト機能による名誉毀損を認めた判決は日本初であるという．

　広告そのものに対する考え方を一新するべきだという批判もある．ソーシャ

ル・ネットワークで広告を発信する際には今までとは異なった発想が必要になってくるからだ．企業の社会的責任についての近著 Who Cares Wins: Why Good Business is Better Business（邦題『正義の会社が勝つ』）の作者 David Jones（デイビット・ジョーンズ）は，ソーシャル・ネットワークの時代には企業が製品情報を完全にコントロールするのではなく，消費者が互いに教えあったり共有したくなったりするようなコンテンツを作成することの方が重要だと主張している．

　participatory consumers の批判的な視線は新聞社や放送局など既存のニュース・メディアにも向けられている．それらのメディアが小手先の広告手法の改善にだけ気を取られていると，モバイル化の波に足をすくわれてしてしまう可能性がある．

英作文問題

　英作文の問題に挑戦してみよう．下記の日本文を英文に訳しなさい．

問題 7. 行動ターゲティングは広告の費用対効果を 10％以上引き上げる．
ヒント．「〜以上」を英語で厳密に言えば at least 〜 であり，more than 〜 ではない．

問題 8. 多くの若者は新聞を読む習慣がない．
ヒント．習慣は habit を使う．

関連語

geo-targeting technology　地域特定技術：ウェブ・サイトの閲覧者の居住地域を，使用 PC の IP アドレスの解析によって特定する技術のこと

consumer propensity　消費性向：可処分所得（所得から税金など非消費支出を差し引いた残り）のうち，消費にあてられる額の割合

conversion rate　顧客転換率：消費者がインターネットのウェブ・サイトで商品やサービスを見て実際に購入に至る割合のこと．購入者数÷訪問者数×100 で算出する（単位は％）．

contextual advertising　コンテンツ連動型広告：ウェブ・サイトに掲載されている情報のキーワードや文脈を自動解析して，その内容と関連性の高い広告を配信するシステムのこと．

banner advertising　バナー広告：ウェブ・サイトに広告の画像やテキストを貼り付けて，それをクリックすると広告主のウェブ・サイトにジャンプする広告手法のこと．

cookie　クッキー：特定のウェブ・サイトを訪れた人が閲覧した情報やアクセス回数などの情報をPCのハードディスクに保存して，次回その人が同一サイトを再訪する時にIDの識別を容易にするためのデータファイルのこと．
CSR　corporate social responsibility：企業の社会的責任のこと．利益追求以外に企業が社会に与える影響について十分な配慮が必要だという考え．
prosumer　プロシューマー：producer（生産者）とconsumer（消費者）を組み合わせた造語で，既存の商品やサービスに満足せず，自らの理想とするアイディアを商品化しようとする消費者のこと．

5．Paywall（有料購読システム）導入の拡大

　広告に次ぐ新聞社の収入源はcirculation revenue（新聞販売収入）である．先述のNAAの調査によると，加盟新聞社の2012年の全収入のうち27%を占めている．これは前年に比べて5%の増加であり，2003年から2011年まで続いていた減少傾向にようやく歯止めがかかった．

　新聞販売状況は決して楽観できる状況ではない．print-only circulation revenue（紙媒体のみの新聞販売収入）に限って見てみると，2012年に14%も減少してしまっているからである．宅配，駅のニューススタンド，アメリカの市街地でよく見かける路上のコイン販売機などで新聞を購入する人が1割以上も減ってしまっている．

　print-only circulation revenueの低迷に悩む新聞社の多くはインターネットと紙面デジタル化技術を活用した新たなビジネス・モデルの構築を急いでいる．その努力はまだまだ彼らの紙媒体の収入源を完全に補うほどの成果をあげてはいないが，一部で明るい兆しが見え始めている．

　アメリカの大手金融情報通信社ブルーンバーグの電子版ニュースレターによると，ニューヨーク・タイムズが2013年2月7日に同社の2012年第4四半期（10月〜12月）の決算結果を公表し，net profit（純利益）が前年同期に比べて約3倍の1億7,691万ドルになったことを明らかにした．

　ニューヨーク・タイムズが好業績をあげた主な要因としては，同紙のpaid digital subscriber（有料デジタル購読者）が予想外に増えたことと，傘下の

About.comやIndeed.comの株式売却益を計上したことが挙げられている．

　ニューヨーク・タイムズは広告収入への高依存体質から脱皮しつつある．同紙とインターナショナル・ヘラルド・トリビューン（ニューヨーク・タイムズがアメリカ国外で発行している英字紙）のpaid digital subscriberは2012年9月以降に13.1％も増加して合計64万人に達した．同社の2012年通年の新聞販売収入は9億5,300万ドルとなり，史上初めて同社の年間広告収入（8億9,810万ドル）を上回った．これにより長らく広告収入の落ち込みに苦しんできたニューヨーク・タイムズが歴史的なターニング・ポイントを迎えた．

　ブルーンバーグによると，新聞・出版業界では健全な収入比率を広告80％に対して販売収入20％と考えてきたが，それはもはや時代遅れになりつつある．

　ニューヨーク・タイムズでは2013年第1四半期（1月〜3月）の予測でもpaid digital subscriberは堅調に増加を続けて，新聞販売収入を前年同期比で4％〜6％押し上げる原動力になると見込んでいる．そうなれば同紙の収入比率における広告収入の割合は今後さらに小さくなっていき，広告需要の変動に左右されにくい安定的な経営につながりそうである．

　ニューヨーク・タイムズがなぜこれほどまでに有料購読者を増やすことができたのだろうか．きっかけは，同紙が2011年3月に導入したpaywallと呼ばれる有料購読システムを導入したことだった．

　paywallとは特定のウェブ・サイトの情報閲覧を有料購読者に限って提供するシステムのことである．ただし，このニューヨーク・タイムズの課金システムでは，すべての記事が有料というわけではない．お金を払わない人はすべて同紙のウェブ・サイトにアクセスさせないという閉鎖的なシステムではない．むしろ，より詳細で質の高いニュースならばたとえお金を払ってでも入手したいという人を「有料プレミアム会員」として待遇し，彼らが望む特別な閲覧サービスを提供するというビジネス・モデルなのである．

　ニューヨーク・タイムズはすぐに有料会員になることをためらう読者に対しては，無料会員登録を勧めている．同紙のウェブ・サイトに名前を登録さえすれば毎月10本の記事までは無料で閲覧できる．それ以上の記事を閲覧したい人は有料会員になればよい．

このような仕組みはmetered model（メーター制課金）と呼ばれていて, ウェブ上のコンテンツを閲覧する際に一定量の情報は無料とし, それを超える場合には有料となる課金制度である.

metered modelは英国の金融・経済専門紙Financial Timesが先駆けて導入したことでよく知られている制度である（FTの場合, 無料登録会員は毎月8本までに記事を閲覧可能である）. ニューヨーク・タイムズのpaywallはFTと同様にmetered modelを採用し, ウェブ・サイトでの閲覧者を緩やかにpaywallへと誘導する作戦が功を奏している.

このpaywallという言葉自体は日本ではまだあまり一般的に認知されていないが, 類似のシステムはすでに朝日新聞や日本経済新聞が導入し, 両社ともに「有料電子版」という呼称を用いている.

筆者は朝日新聞の有料電子版を利用しているが,「無料会員は閲覧できる記事数に制限があります」というメッセージが表示されることから, 朝日新聞の電子版もmetered modelを採用していることが分かる.

朝日新聞電子版利用者としての筆者の個人的感想ではあるが, 有料記事閲覧サービスのメリットは大きいと感じている. 特に出張などで自宅を留守にする際にはホテルなどでインターネットが使える環境があれば, スマートフォン, タブレット型コンピューター, ノート・パソコンを使ってデジタル化された新聞紙面がすぐに読め, 気になる記事は電子的にクリップして会員のウェブ・サイト上に記録しておけるからである. 海外に出かける際にもこれらの機能は国内にいる時と同様に利用できるので非常に便利である.

ニューヨーク・タイムズの好決算に関して, もう一つ注目すべきことは, 有料デジタル購読者の数が増加しても, 紙媒体の読者が減らないということである. これはデジタル購読と紙媒体購読は競合せず, むしろ互いを補完し合う関係になりうることを示している. つまり, 新聞のhome delivery（宅配）を受けている人が追加的にpaid digital subscriberにもなって会社や出張先でモバイル情報端末を使って記事を閲覧するケースが増えている.

このような相互補完関係が成立している背景にはニューヨーク・タイムズが紙の新聞購読とデジタル購読の両方を契約している人に対して購読料の割引サービ

スなどの優遇措置を行っているという事実も見逃せない．このような優遇サービスはニューヨーク・タイムズ以外にも多くの新聞社がすでに導入し，ある程度の相乗効果を挙げている．

ピュー・リサーチ・センターの調査によると，アメリカの 1,380 の日刊紙のうち，450 紙が paywall をすでに導入している．そして，新聞業界全体の print and digital bundled circulation revenue（紙媒体とデジタル版の抱合せ販売収入）は 2012 年に 499％ も増加している．これは digital-only circulation revenue（デジタル版のみの販売収入）の 275％ 増を大きく上回るハイペースな上昇である．

その一方で print-only circulation（紙媒体のみの販売収入）は 14％ も減少しているので，紙媒体だけに固執する新聞社はますます苦しい状況に置かれているのも事実である．

新聞業界では紙面デジタル化にいち早く取り組んで紙媒体とデジタル版の抱合せ販売を行っている新聞社は勝ち組になり，対照的に，デジタル化に躊躇して紙媒体のみを提供している新聞社は負け組になるという二極化が進行しつつある．そのため，ほとんどの新聞社は生き残りをかけて紙面デジタル化に今後なお一層力を入れていくことが予想される．paywall の導入が新聞業界全体に拡大する可能性が高い．

paywall を導入しても，すべての新聞社が有料購読者を順調に獲得できるとは限らない．新聞社によって読者を惹きつける能力に大きな格差があるからである．

英作文問題
　英作文の問題に挑戦してみよう．下記の日本文を英文に訳しなさい．

問題 9. 新規事業では新聞販売収入の落ち込みを埋め合わせできない．
　ヒント．「～を埋め合わせする」は make up for ～ を使う

問題 10. 有料デジタル購読者が予想外に増えた．
　ヒント．「予想外に増えた」は increased faster than expected を使える．

関連語

online free membership　オンライン無料会員：インターネット上で提供されているサービスのすべてまたは一部を一定期間無料で受けられる権利．

native advertising　ネイティブ広告：ウェブ・サイト上で，一見広告らしくなく記事のような構成でつくられている広告のこと．advertising（広告）とeditorial（記事）を合わせた造語advertorial（アドバトリアル＝記事体広告）とも呼ばれる．

freemium　フリーミアム：基本的なサービスや製品を無料提供し，高度なオプション機能について料金を課金する仕組みのこと．free（無料）とpremium（割増料金）を合成して作った言葉．

brand loyalty　ブランド忠実度：消費者が特定のブランドを信望して購入し続けること．

6. news app（ニュース閲覧専用アプリ）でより多くの購読者囲い込みを図る大手メディア

　news consumersは何を基準にしてニュース閲覧サイトを選別しているのだろうか．最近の調査によって，スマートフォンやタブレットPCなどのモバイル情報端末を使用しているnews consumersはニュース・メディアを選別する際に興味深い特性があることが分かってきた．

　ピュー・リサーチ・センター（2012）によると，彼らは知名度や信頼度の高いニュース・メディアのウェブ・サイトに繰り返しアクセスする傾向が強い．その理由は，大手の著名なニュース・メディアが自社のウェブ・サイトになるべく多くのnews consumersを誘導するために開発したnews app（ニュース閲覧専用アプリ）をオンラインで無料配布しているからである．

　たとえば，ニューヨーク・タイムズはNYTimesというアプリを無料でオンライン配布している．利用者はニューヨーク・タイムズのトップ・ニュース・セクションだけを無料で閲覧できるが，有料購読者になると全25セクションの記事をオンラインで閲覧できるようになる．

　news appはモバイル情報端末の液晶タッチパネル上でアイコンに軽く触れるだけでニュース・メディアのサイトを即座に表示してくれるので，使い勝手が良い．PCを起動してウェブ・ブラウザを起ち上げるよりも短時間でニュースを閲覧することができる．

　news consumersは複数の大手メディアのnews appを利用している人が多く，

それらを用いて頻繁にニュースを閲覧する傾向にある．彼らのオンライン上の行動は検索サイトからニュースに触れることが多いデスクトップ・パソコンのユーザーとは初動が異なる．

　大手ニュース・メディアにはもう一つの強みがある．それは，国外のニュース購読者を惹きつけるブランド力である．アメリカのメディア・アナリストで今は無きアメリカの大手通信社ナイトリッダーの記者を経験した Ken Doctor（ケン・ドクター）が運営する NEWSONOMICS.Com によると，ニューヨーク・タイムズの paid digital subscriber のうち約 10％がアメリカ国外に住む人である．

　時間や地域の制約を気にせずにニューヨーク・タイムズの報道にフル・アクセスしたい国外居住者にとって news app を使ってのニュース閲覧は非常に使い勝手が良い．

　news app には注意すべき点もある．特定のニュース・メディアのウェブ・サイトばかりを閲覧する機会が増えるので，ニュースの内容によっては偏った解釈や立場のみを目にする危険性がある．

英作文問題

　英作文の問題に挑戦してみよう．下記の日本文を英文に訳しなさい．

問題 11. ニュース閲覧専用アプリによって大手ニュース・メディアは多くの有料購読者を獲得することができる．

ヒント．動詞は enable を使うと日本語の語順に沿ったシンプルな英文になります．

関連語

App Store　アップ・ストア：iPhone，iPad などアップル社製のモバイル情報端末のために app（アプリケーション）を販売する同社のオンライン・ショップ．

Google Play　グーグル・プレイ：Google 社のアンドロイド OS を搭載したモバイル情報端末のためにアプリを販売する同社のオンライン・ショップ．

7. 新聞の未来

　NAAによると，2011年時点でアメリカの日刊紙は朝刊が931紙，夕刊が451紙，日曜版が900紙だった．総発行部数は朝刊が約4,032万部，夕刊が410万部，日曜版が4,851万部だった．今後，新聞のデジタル化はますます進むだろうが，近い将来にこれらの新聞がすべてなくなってしまう可能性は低い．

　しかし，新聞の未来について多くの懸念材料があることも事実であり，新聞社がそれと真摯に向き合っていかなければ多くの新聞が読者を失うことになる．

　報道の質は低下してきている．2013年4月26日の『朝日新聞』朝刊は，ボストン・マラソンで起きた爆破テロ事件の際にアメリカのメディアによる誤報の連鎖が起きたことを報じている．CNNの犯人誤認報道を契機に，ボストン・グローブ紙，全米TVネットワーク局のフォックス・ニュース，AP通信などが勇み足をしてしまったのである．

　CNNとフォックス・ニュースは2012年6月にも医療保険改革法に関する最高裁判決の結果を逆に報道した．

　この朝日新聞の記事は，TwitterやFacebookが誤報を拡散させたと指摘している．ソーシャル・ネットワークが新聞の代わりを務めることはできないことは明らかである．

　先述のピュー・リサーチ・センターが2013年3月13日に発表した3,000人を対象に行った世論調査の結果によると，彼らの31%が報道の質が低下したために，ニュース・メディアのウェブ・サイトを見なくなったと回答している．

　セキュリティやプライバシーの問題もある．新聞のデジタル化やモバイル化がさらに進めば，新聞購読者の個人情報を守る技術もいっそう強化していかなければならない．

　新聞購読者の高齢化も進んでいる．この問題の解決は容易ではないので，地道に対処していくためには若者の知恵を借りなければならないであろう．結局，新聞の未来は若者に託すしかない．

参考文献

「GoogleのQ4決算は36%増収，年間売上高が初の500億ドル超え」，ITpro，2013年1月23日，http://itpro.nikkeibp.co.jp/article/NEWS/20130123/451302/

「日本は業務のモバイル化が遅れている．ワークスタイルの実態調査で明らかに」，Wired日本語版ウェブ・サイト，2013年3月12日，http://wired.jp/2013/03/12/byod-vmware/

スティーブン・レヴィ[仲達志，池村千秋訳]『グーグル ネット覇者の真実：追われる立場から追う立場へ』（毎日コミュニケーションズ，2011）

デイビット・ジョーンズ『正義の会社が勝つ』（ピアソン桐原，2012）

"The American Newspaper Media Industry Revenue Profile 2012," April 8, 2013, http://www.naa.org/Trends-and-Numbers/Newspaper-Revenue/Newspaper-Media-Industry-Revenue-Profile-2012.aspx

"The State of News Media 2012—An Annual Report on American Journalism: Mobile Devices and News Consumption: Some Good Signs for Journalism," Survey Reports, March 20, 2012,
http://stateofthemedia.org/2012/mobile-devices-and-news-consumption-some-good-signs-for-journalism/

"The State of News Media 2013—An Annual Report on American Journalism: Newspapers: Stabilizing, but Still Threatened," Survey Reports, March 18, 2013, http://stateofthemedia.org/2013/newspapers-stabilizing-but-still-threatened/

解答

問題1　The Internet made news search much easier.
問題2　Smartphone ownership exceeded 50% in 2013.
問題3　An increasing number of people have started using smartphones.
問題4　Android users outnumbered iPhone users.
問題5　Print advertising made up 46% of the total revenue of the newspaper industry.
問題6　Classified advertising is convenient for small and midsize companies.
問題7　Behavioral targeting raises the cost effectiveness of advertisements by at least 10%.
問題8　Many young people do not have the habit of reading newspapers.
問題9　New businesses can't make up for a decline in circulation revenue.
問題10　Paid digital subscribers increased faster than expected.
問題11　News apps enable major news media to get many paid digital subscribers.

第3章

アメリカの憲法と社会

はじめに

アメリカでは，政治や社会のさまざまな場面で，憲法が話題になります．この章では，アメリカにとってなぜ憲法が重要なのか，歴史的な説明をし，人種問題・妊娠中絶権論争・同性婚問題を例に，憲法がどのように社会的論争の焦点になってきたのかを紹介します．そのうえで自由や民主主義というアメリカの理念を体現する合衆国憲法の普遍性について考えます．

以下の英文を読み，各セクションのReview Questionsで内容確認しましょう．

1. The U.S. Constitution: The Most Important Promise

(1) The Presidential Oath
When the U.S. President is elected, a great inauguration ceremony is held in Washington D.C., where the President is sworn into office by taking the Presidential Oath. In front of a flag-waving audience of hundreds of thousands of people, the President places his (so far all the Presidents have been male) hand on the Bible and says these words:

"*I do solemnly swear that I will faithfully execute the Office of President of the United States, and will to the best of my Ability, preserve, protect and defend the Constitution of the United States.*"

Thus, the first and foremost duty of the President of the United States is to "preserve, protect and defend the Constitution of the United States." Why is the Constitution so important to the people of the United States?

(2) The U.S. Constitution = the U.S. itself

By 1776, conditions had become ripe for the British colonies in North America to demand independence from the King. Thomas Jefferson penned the now famous words of the *Declaration of Independence*, asserting that "all men are created equal" and that people were born with rights which the government had to protect. The colonists thought that the British King had been disrespectful of their rights, and declared their intent to become independent.

After the Independence War with Great Britain and the first experiment with their own government (Articles of Confederation), the former colonies decided to unite under a new form of government—the United States of America. The U.S. Constitution was a document that established this government—setting its basic rules, such as the role of different parts of the government and the rights of the people.

Therefore, the U.S. Constitution is the United States itself. The United States was literally established by this document, as a promise between the people of the 13 states to become a nation. Its political image, ideals and identity were created, and continues to be recreated, under the bonds formed by this promise. The U.S. Constitution, drafted in 1787, is still effective today. It is one of the longest living constitutions in the world.

(3) What does the Constitution include?

The U.S. Constitution consists of 7 Articles (Article I through VII), the Bill of Rights (The first ten amendments), and subsequent amendments.

The Articles focus on the powers of the government. Article I is about the legislature (Congress) that enacts laws reflecting the basic policies of the nation. Article II is about the executive branch (President) that executes the law and conducts foreign policy. Article III is about the judiciary (the courts) that adjudicates legal disputes. The colonies declared independence from the King because they were dissatisfied with how the King governed them. So these Articles, setting the rules for how the United States should be governed, were most important to the Founders who wrote the Constitution.

The Bill of Rights was added to make sure that the government would not violate rights that the Founders thought were important. The First Amendment is most famous, as it protects civil liberties such as freedom of speech, freedom of religion, freedom of the press and freedom of assembly. These freedoms are essential to democracy as well as to individuals.

The U.S. Constitution also reserved significant powers to the states. This form of government is called federalism. For example, family laws, which determine who can marry whom, depend on each state. States like Massachusetts allow same-sex marriage, but most other states do not. States tend to prefer preserving the power to enact laws on their own, so there have been frequent battles between the states and the federal government over who should prevail.

The U.S. Constitution allows for amendments in order to respond to changes in the nation. Amendments are added after the existing document.

The most significant amendments were ratified after the Civil War between the Northern and Southern states. The U.S. Constitution prior to the Civil War allowed slavery. Maintenance of slavery was considered essential to Southern economy (especially for the expansion of cotton plantations) and way of life, but the North, which continued to grow in industry and finance, gradually adopted the cause of abolition.

As a result of the Civil War, which ended in Northern victory, the 13th Amendment, which abolished slavery, was ratified. Further, the 14th Amendment, which among other things called for "equal protection of the laws" (the government cannot discriminate between people) was ratified. The 15th

Amendment prohibited discrimination in voting on account of race.

(4) Constitutional conflicts and the role of courts

If someone thinks that his or her right under the Constitution is being violated by the government, this person can ask for the intervention of the court. The court can decide whether or not there is a violation, and order a remedy (or even void the actions of other branches of the government) if there is. This role of the court is called judicial review.

However, this task is not easy, because the meaning of the Constitution is not always clear. For example, the 14th Amendment protects equality. Today, same-sex couples are demanding the right to marry, arguing that under the right to equality, they should be able to marry each other just like heterosexual (male-female) couples. Both the courts and the U.S. society is divided over the answer to this question.

Some people criticize the fact that the court, consisting of a small number of judges who are not elected by the people, is making such important decisions. But when courts take up important issues such as same-sex marriage, they do not rush to decision. The conflicts are first brought to the lower courts, and it is only after the issues have been debated over and over in the lower courts that it moves on to a higher level, and ultimately to the highest level, the Supreme Court of the United States.

By the time it gets to the Supreme Court, the issue will have been debated intensely throughout the nation, in the press and in various citizens' meetings, in street demonstrations and in the halls of state assemblies as well as Congress. In a sense, the democratic process is activated by people raising constitutional issues and asking for the intervention of the courts. The Supreme Court is the final decision-maker, but not the only actor, in deciding the meaning of the Constitution. The entire nation is involved.

This is why the U.S. Constitution can be said to be owned by, and important to, the people of the United States.

Review Questions
1. In your own words, discuss why the U.S. Constitution is "the most important promise".
2. Why are courts important in the U.S.?

2. Equality: Race in U.S. Society

I have a dream that my four little children will one day live in a nation where they will not be judged by the color of their skin but by the content of their character.

I have a dream today!
—Martin Luther King, Jr. "I Have a Dream" speech (1963)

(1) Racial segregation in the U.S.

Do you know what an American school bus looks like? May be you have seen it on TV or in the movies, or in person if you have travelled to the U.S. It is yellow, with black stripes running across both sides, and may come with a built-in "stop" sign to warn other cars when children are boarding or getting off. It may have the name of the school or the school district printed on its side. The bus may be large, or it may be smaller, like a mini-van. The school bus is a common feature of American school life, and can be seen in almost any town in the United States.

But did you know that the school bus carries with it much history and conflict, and the "dreams" of Americans with it? The school bus is a symbol of racial integration—or perhaps, a symbol of *hopes* of integration while at the same time representing the reality of the U.S.—that people of different races still tend to live apart and go to different schools.

The U.S. has a long history of racial segregation, which is to keep different races apart. Racial segregation was *strengthened* after the abolishment of slavery, as if to reinforce the differences between races.

Separate schools were created for whites and blacks, so that black children cannot go to white childrens' school even if that school was closer to home. Public facilities, such as transportation, hotels, restaurants, and even movie theaters, were segregated by race. On trains, black people had to sit in designated cars. In the bus, they had to sit in the back. At movie theaters, whites and blacks had to enter through a different door, and sit in different areas according to their race.

This was not just about blacks. In San Francisco, an "oriental school" for Chinese people was established. In 1905, San Francisco tried to order all Japanese students to go to this separate school too, reflecting the anti-Japanese sentiment then rising in California. Tension between the U.S. and Japan arose as a result, and after a series of negotiations involving the U.S. President, San Francisco rescinded this policy, while the Japanese government agreed to voluntarily limit Japanese immigration to the U.S.

In 1896, one case challenging legally-mandated segregation came up to the U.S. Supreme Court. Mr. Plessy, who was seven-eighths white and one-eighth black, intentionally sat in a train car reserved for whites and was arrested for violating the law. Although Mr. Plessy was mixed-blooded and his appearance was white, according to the law he was black, based on the "one-drop rule" that legally defined a person as black if he or she had even one ancestor that was black. The U.S. Supreme Court rejected Mr. Plessy's claim, arguing that segregation was not discrimination. The Court believed that equality can be achieved without people of different races associating with each other. This came to be called the "separate but equal" doctrine.

But the reality was not "separate but equal". Blacks were separated from whites, and treated in an inferior (unequal) manner. Facilities for whites were better than facilities for blacks, if the latter had a facility at all.

(2) The beginnings of change

During World War II, Japanese and Japanese Americans residing in California, Oregon and Washington were taken away from their homes and placed in internment camps constructed far away, in deserts and in the mountains (this will be discussed later in this chapter).

Ironically, the second generation children in the internment camps were asked to join the U.S. Army despite their treatment as "enemy aliens". When they joined to prove their loyalty to the U.S., they were segregated into units solely composed of Japanese Americans—the most famous being the 442nd. Regimental Combat Team. This Japanese American unit came to be the most decorated unit in the U.S. Army, winning a recognition from the U.S. President following the war.

In 1948, President Truman issued an order to desegregate the armed forces, despite strong opposition from within the military.

Times were changing. Building on this trend came the Civil Rights Movement—the mass mobilization of black people as well as white people who wanted change, calling for racial equality and racial integration.

In 1954, in a landmark decision called *Brown v. Board of Education*, the U.S. Supreme Court surprised the nation by reversing the *Plessy* decision of 1896. Chief Justice Earl Warren wrote that separate schools based on race could never be equal. Children will come to know that the reason behind segregation was the view that black children were inferior. This sense of inferiority will harm them psychologically, and will result in a disadvantage for the rest of their lives.

While some cheered the Court's new direction, others fiercely resisted. In Little Rock, Arkansas (1957), the governor tried to prevent the integration of a local high school by sending state troops to block black children from entering the school. Ultimately, President Eisenhower decided to send in federal troops to protect the black children. School integration had to be achieved by military force.

(3) Martin Luther King's "Dream"

In 1963, nearly a decade after the *Brown* decision, Martin Luther King, Jr. made one of the most famous speeches in U.S. history at "The Mall" in Washington D.C.—the place where Presidential Inauguration Ceremonies are held. This was at the height of the Civil Rights Movement. After reciting the injustices of segregation and discrimination committed against black people, Martin Luther King called on the nation to join in his dream of racial integration. He wanted to see a day when his children would be able to join hands with white children "as sisters and brothers."

In 2008, the first black President, Barack Obama was elected, and proudly held his inauguration ceremony at the same place that Martin Luther King spoke. Was this a dream come true? Some bemoan the fact that the U.S. society still seems to be divided along the lines of race.

Where does the school bus come in? It is in the effort to integrate schools—to have children of different races study together, that the school bus became widely utilized across the U.S. In the U.S., people of different races have tended to live in different neighborhoods. How could you "mix" children of different races when they live apart? One answer was to use the school bus to carry children from different neighborhoods to the same schools so they can interact with each other.

The school bus is a sign that many Americans did take the Court's decision to integrate schools, and Martin Luther King's dream, seriously. It was a tremendous undertaking for schools across the nation to come up with a system of busing children everyday.

At the same time, this effort caused much opposition and protracted battles. In places like South Boston, armed police officers had to guard the buses to prevent angry crowds from attacking them. Others have gone to the courts to argue that forced busing was a violation of *their* rights and that it should not be required.

When you see the yellow school bus in the U.S., hopefully you will think of the dreams and conflicts behind this seemingly innocent creature.

Review questions
1. How was racial segregation applied to blacks (African Americans) and Japanese (Japanese Americans) in the U.S.?
2. Is forcing racial integration by using school buses a good solution or is there a better solution?

3. Privacy: Personal Matters or Not?

(1) The abortion debate

The U.S. Constitution touches many peoples' lives in personal ways too. One issue that has raised strong sentiments is the right of women to choose whether or not to give birth to a child after having become pregnant. This is the abortion rights controversy.

Abortion is a difficult issue. It is a very personal matter for the mother, whose life will be most affected by the choice of whether or not to have children. But it may also be a matter that is important to the father, who will also be affected by that choice, and even parents (for example, if the mother is an unwed teenager who is dependent on them). Some hold deeply religious views against abortion—that life begins at the time of conception, and that artificially terminating that life is not much different from murder.

In *Roe v. Wade* (1973), the Supreme Court chose to take up this complex issue as a matter of rights. There is no provision in the U.S. Constitution that explicitly protects a women's right to have abortion. But the Court "found" such a right by interpreting the Constitution, coming up with the right to privacy, and deciding that this right could be extended to the choice of having an abortion.

(2) The right to privacy

Privacy here has a broad meaning. One jurist (Justice Louis Brandeis) used the expression "the right to be left alone." It includes the many personal choices that a person makes in his or her lives.

Many of the Court's decisions regarding the right to privacy have had to do with procreation. *Griswold v. Connecticut* (1965), considered as the pioneering case, was about the use of contraceptives. The law of that state prohibited the use of contraceptives, and not only did it punish those who used them, it also punished those who taught others how to use them.

In *Griswold*, the Supreme Court held that the U.S. Constitution implicitly recognized the right to privacy. The U.S. Constitution contained many provisions that were based on the idea that people should be free from government intrusion. Freedom of speech was based on the idea that the government should not be able to control people's minds. Rights regarding criminal procedure (the Fourth Amendment) limit the government's authority to search people's homes or to seize their property.

If so, the Court asked, should the government be able to search a married couples' bedroom and see if they have been using contraceptives? The Court determined that such a law intrudes upon the right to privacy, and is therefore invalid. In the worldview of the U.S. Constitution, individuals have a private sphere—whether they be the mind, the home, or the choices they make—that the government cannot intrude upon without good reason and proper procedures.

(3) Roe and its aftermath: "pro-choice" and "pro-life"

While *Roe v. Wade* has been held up as a landmark case for "pro-choice" people (those advocating the right of women to decide to have abortion), it also led to the emergence of "pro-life" people (those who feel that abortion is undesirable and should be restricted).

In some states, those who opposed abortion engaged in intense demonstrations against abortion clinics (doctors who conducted abortion) and succeeded in shutting them down.

Not only was there public resistance to the idea of a right to abortion, but many states tried to discourage abortion despite the Supreme Court decision. The Supreme Court granted the right of women to decide to have abortion in principle, but also left some room for regulation or restriction. The states have since enacted regulations that were meant to make it more difficult to have abortion. This included, for example, the requirement to obtain permission from husbands, or parents in the case of minors; mandatory counseling (which may include showing the mother pictures of the child in her womb and thereby discouraging abortion); and 24-hour waiting periods (which would require the women to rethink and come back later).

Bowing to intense public pressure, and also because of the changes within the Court, the Supreme Court upheld most of these regulations in a 1992 decision (*Casey case*).

Recent debates have been over late-term abortion. The later it is in pregnancy, the more the baby will have taken the shape and functions of human beings. There is a chance that the baby will be able to survive if taken out of the mother's womb. Is abortion permissible under such conditions, or is it the same as murder? What if the mother's life was at risk if she were to continue her pregnancy? Would you risk the mother's life, or would you allow the baby to be "aborted"?

These are the questions that are being asked over abortion. To some it is not even a question of the Constitution, but of their religion or moral values. To others it is an important constitutional right.

Review questions
1. Pretend that you are "pro-choice" and "pro-life". Summarize the main arguments on both sides.
2. Do you think that abortion is a constitutional right? What kind of regulation (or restriction) is permissible?

4. Liberty: Limiting Government Power

In framing a government which is to be administered by men over men, the great difficulty lies in this: you must first enable the government to control the governed; and in the next place oblige it to control itself.
—James Madison, in *Federalist Papers, No. 51*

(1) Freedom of speech and democracy

Democracy is a form of government that Americans cherish. It is based on the idea that the government is made of ordinary people, not by a separate class of people such as aristocrats. It is also based on the idea that government is to act for the welfare of ordinary people, instead of for the few people who are in power.

Democracy in practice takes the form of majoritarian decision-making in the popularly elected legislature. Members of Congress, who represent the people's will, deliberate and vote on issues and enact them into law.

However, there is danger in democracy too, if it is unchecked. Democratic government can be as tyrannical as a dictator if the will of the majority can do anything to the lives of people. This is especially so during times of excitement or fear, when people may lose sight and call for extreme solutions.

This is why preservation of individual liberty becomes an important concern. "Individual" liberty means that individuals have certain rights that must be protected, even if it is opposed to the interests of the majority.

A good example of this is freedom of speech, protected under the First Amendment of the U.S. Constitution. Freedom of speech is essential both for the individual and for a functional democracy. It is important for the individual because what makes human beings different from each other and from other animals is the capacity to read, write, learn and think, and to express themselves. Freedom of speech gives us the capacity to become dignified human beings with individuality.

Freedom of speech is also essential for democracy. Democracy rests on the premise that people make the choice as to what their government should do. But how can people make a choice if there is a lack of choices, or if they cannot understand the consequences of different choices? In order for the people to be able to make *real* choices, a free, lively discussion of all the choices that are available, including criticizing and making comparisons with current government policies, is critical. Freedom of speech is guaranteed to encourage such discussion. It is the foundation of democracy and the American style of government.

(2) Dividing government power to protect liberty

The Founders also came up with an indirect way of protecting individual liberties. They established several competing branches within the government, each strong and independent enough to compete with each other. Because of this competition, no one will be able to do everything that he or she wants to do. This is the idea of separation of powers.

People from other countries have the image of a strong, visible U.S. President. But in fact, the U.S. President's power is limited. He cannot propose and enact a law. Only Congress can. Further, the Congress and the President are elected separately by the people, so they may have different opinions depending on when the people elected them and under what circumstances. For example, the Republican party may be a majority in Congress, while the President may be from the Democratic party. The result is that the Congress and President may frequently disagree over important policy issues.

The President cannot always get what he wants because it is Congress that decides domestic policy. He can persuade Congress or apply pressure on Congress by going public and gaining the support of the people. It may take much time, and it may still be unsuccessful. Some may think that this is frustratingly inefficient. But this is the whole point of separation of powers. It makes sure that the government is careful, that important decisions should only be made when different actors with different opinions agree. In the end, this prevents the government from making hasty decisions based on a one-sided view.

The Constitution, in addition to dividing powers between different branches of the government, gives each branch the ability to check the actions of other branches in order to prevent any abuse of power ("checks and balances").

We have already talked about judicial review—the power of the courts to review and void the actions of other branches if they violate the Constitution.

Another well-known example is the veto power of the President. If the President refuses to sign a law passed by Congress, the law cannot take effect. This enables the President to block laws which he thinks do not respond to public opinion, or thinks is hastily crafted. If the President vetoes a bill, Congress needs to come up with a *two-thirds* majority, which usually means that it has to take into consideration opinions of both the majority and minority party in Congress. Thus, abuses by the majority in Congress can be prevented in this way.

On the other hand, Congress can check the powers of the President in several ways. For example, when the President wants to appoint important members of the federal government, such as Justices of the Supreme Court and ambassadors to foreign countries, he needs to get the consent of the Senate. The President has the power to negotiate with foreign countries and sign treaties, but in order for such treaties to take effect, again, he needs to have the consent of the Senate. In this manner, the Senate serves as a check on Presidential power.

(3) Times of emergency and concerns about power

The government faces a dilemma during times of emergency, for example during war, in the midst of terrorist attacks, or even during economic crises and breakouts of diseases. It is during these times that people get excited or frustrated, and demand immediate action from the government. But it is also during these times that there is a danger of abuses of power and violation of rights.

A moment in U.S. history where this dilemma became most evident involves the Japanese people. During World War II, fear rose among some people within the U.S. military, that the many Japanese immigrants and their offspring that were residing in the West Coast—the states of Washington, Oregon and California—might cooperate with the Japanese military in the event of a Japanese attack on the U.S. mainland.

The stereotypical view that all Japanese were potential enemies of the U.S. led to the idea of removing them from the West Coast. As a result, an estimated 110,000 residents of Japanese ancestry were forced into internment camps that were built in isolated locations in the interior—such as in the midst of deserts in Arizona and New Mexico, and in the mountains of Colorado. Yet, in Hawaii, where Pearl Harbor was *actually* attacked by the Japanese forces, only a small group of Japanese leaders were detained, not the entire Japanese population.

Some people resisted internment, arguing that they were Americans and that they should be treated as Americans, with full constitutional rights. This included people like Fred Korematsu, who tried to evade internment by having plastic surgery; and Gordon Hirabayashi, a college student who intentionally violated the curfew order and walked into a police station to get arrested, so that he can go to the court and argue that the treatment of Japanese Americans was a violation of the U.S. Constitution.

Here, the Court faced the dilemma. Should it respect the judgments of the military, the President and Congress, which supported the internment under the situation of a war with Japan? Or should it protect individual rights under the Constitution? Mr. Hirabayashi and Mr. Korematsu were loyal American citizens, although their parents were Japanese. They were born in, and grew up in, the United States, and had little attachment to Japan.

The majority of the Court decided to side with the military. In the *Hirabayashi* case (1943), the Court took the position that, because the government cannot readily distinguish between loyal Japanese and disloyal Japanese, it was reasonable to take measures against all persons of Japanese ancestry.

But an important new trend emerged in the *Korematsu* case (1944). Several dissenting judges emerged to criticize the majority opinion, with Justice Murphy declaring that the internment "falls into the ugly abyss of racism". If enemy aliens were dangerous, why not the Germans and Italians, who were also enemies in this war? Murphy pointed out that only the Japanese were being treated this way and that this was an act of racial discrimination.

While the constitutional rights of Japanese Americans were sacrificed during World War II, the cases they brought to the Court left an important legacy as shown in the following episode.

In the aftermath of the September 11 terrorist attacks of 2001 in New York and Washington D.C., President Bush launched several military campaigns abroad in the name of combating terrorism. A detention camp was established in Guantanamo Bay, Cuba to detain those whom the U.S. government considered dangerous.

An inmate who was a U.S. citizen brought a claim to the court, arguing that he was being wrongfully detained, and that he should be given a fair hearing to contest his detention. That is what the constitution requires in ordinary criminal trials—before the government can detain or punish a person for a crime, a fair trial should be held to determine if there is sufficient evidence. This is meant to prevent an innocent person from being wrongfully prosecuted and is called the "due process of the law".

It seems that the Court learned from the experiences of Japanese Americans during World War II. In *Hamdi v. Rumsfeld* (2004), the Court built upon the dissenting opinions in the *Korematsu* case. "A state of war is not a blank check for the President," Justice Sandra Day O'Connor declared. It should not be difficult for the government to conduct individual hearings for those who were detained in Guantanamo Bay, to see if there was sufficient reason for their detention. Even during times of emergency, constitutional rights should not be given away so easily. The Constitution should continue to serve as a check on government power.

Review questions
1. What are the values of freedom of speech?
2. How is the structure of the government related to protection of liberty? Is it the same in your country?
3. Where do you think the balance between government power and individual rights should be during times of emergency?

5. Conclusion: Constitutional Democracy in the U.S.

Finally, the U.S. Constitution is not just important to the people of the United States, but it has also been a model for the world.

This is perhaps due to the peculiar nature of Americans—that they have a missionary zeal to be a "model" for the world when it comes to political and economic ideas, and the systems and rules that are meant to implement those ideas. This has been the case for the ideas of democracy and the rule of law, and so too for the idea of constitutionalism. Americans like to spread these ideas to other countries, and tend to measure other countries in terms of how close they conform to these ideas.

The idea that the government should be based on the will of the people is at the heart of American political ideals. At the same time, Americans have also learned that government power, even if it is based on democratic principles, should be constrained by constitutional limits. Without such constraints, the rights of individuals may be trumped over by a temporary majority. Short-sighted excitement can cause enduring damage to the nation if it is not sufficiently checked. Thus, democracy that abides by the Constitution—constitutional democracy, is provided for by the U.S. Constitution.

The Constitution is alive in U.S. society because the people take it seriously, and when ordinary citizens feel that their constitutional rights—whether the right to equality, privacy, or liberty—are in danger, they are ready to raise constitutional challenges. The ensuing public debate ensures that many people are reminded of, and are involved in, the evolution of constitutional ideas within the society.

Review question
Do you think that the U.S. Constitution can be a model for other countries and societies? Why / why not?

Sample responses for the review questions
Section 1
1. The U.S. Constitution established the United States, and reflects the historical experience of British colonial rule and the political ideals derived from it. It represents the political identity of the United States.
2. The courts have a responsibility to ensure that the government actually acts according to the Constitution. If any part of the government violates the Constitution, the courts have the power to void that action. This power of the courts is called judicial review.

Section 2
1. Despite the 14th Amendment which guaranteed "equal protection of the laws," blacks were segregated from whites by law until the Court finally reversed the "separate but equal

doctrine" in 1954 (*Brown v. Board of Education*). But even after *Brown*, segregation has continued in practice, though it is not forced by the law. The Japanese were also targets of segregation, but in 1905 they successfully resisted the attempt by San Francisco to segregate Japanese school children through the intervention of the U.S. President and the Japanese government.

2. This question asks for your own thoughts. On busing, those in favor may say that it is an effective way to bring children of different races together, while those against may say that forced busing violates their rights to decide on their own education.

Section 3

1. Your own arguments are expected. As an example, a pro-choice person may argue that giving birth to a child affects the mother's life the most, so her choice should be most respected. A pro-life person may argue that the father also has an interest, and also that abortion is about terminating a baby's life, so it should never be an easy option.

2. Your own thinking is expected. On regulation, do you agree with requiring the husband's consent, or parental consent for minors? How about mandatory counseling and waiting periods? Can the government prohibit all late-term abortions, even if the mother's life is at risk?

Section 4

1. Freedom of speech is valuable for the development of human beings with individuality through allowing self-expression. It is essential to democracy because democracy assumes that people have real choices to make. People should be able to express different views and propose alternative ideas, including those that are critical of current policies.

2. In the U.S., the Founders thought about protecting liberty by designing a government structure in which power is divided among many actors. Those actors were to check each other, so that no one will be able to abuse power.

3. This question asks for your own thoughts. Consider, for example, the internment of Japanese Americans during World War II or detention of suspected terrorists at Guantanamo Bay following the September 11 attacks.

Section 5

This question asks for your own thoughts based on your understanding of the U.S. model. For example, do you think that an active role for the courts is desirable? Should power be separated among many government actors, even if it leads to conflicts, tension and inefficiency between them?

参考文献

Cottrol, Robert J., Raymond T. Diamond, and Leland B. Ware, *Brown v. Board of Education: Caste, Culture, and the Constitution* (University Press of Kansas, 2003).

Hamilton, Alexander, James Madison, and John Jay, *The Federalist Papers*.

Hull, N.E.H. and Peter Charles Hoffer, *Roe v. Wade: The Abortion Rights Controversy in American History* (University Press of Kansas, 2001).

McCloskey, Robert G., *The American Supreme Court* [3rd edition] (The University of Chicago Press, 2000).

tenBroek, Jacobus, Edward N. Barnhart, and Floyd W. Matson, *Prejudice, War and the Constitution: Causes and Consequences of the Evacuation of the Japanese Americans in World War II* (University of California Press, 1954).

第4章

アメリカ移民の現状
—— ヒスパニック系を事例に ——

はじめに

第4章では，アメリカ国勢調査局とピュー・ヒスパニック・センターの報告書を読み，その内容を理解することで，アメリカ移民の現状について学ぶ．各セクションの理解度を確認するために，設問を付した．

1. Foreign-born Populations in the United States – 2010

アメリカ合衆国は，世界からさまざまな人びとが集まる「人種のるつぼ」と呼ばれています．アメリカ政府は1790年から10年ごとに，アメリカの人口に関するデータを集めており，この業務を担っている政府組織はアメリカ国勢調査局 (The Bureau of Census) です．アメリカ国勢調査は，アメリカの人口を知る上で重要なデータです．アメリカ国勢調査局の報告書を読み，2010年のアメリカ合衆国の移民人口について学びましょう．

This report presents a portrait of the foreign-born population in the United States. The U.S. Census Bureau uses the term *foreign born* to refer to anyone who is not a U.S. citizen at birth. This includes naturalized citizens, lawful permanent residents, temporary migrants (such as foreign students), humanitarian migrants (such as refugees), and undocumented migrants. The term *native born* refers to anyone born in the United States, Puerto Rico, or a U.S. Island Area, or those born abroad of at least one U.S. citizen parent. Information on the demographic, social, economic, and housing characteristics presented in this report is based on data from the 2010 American Community Survey (ACS). In this report, data on the foreign born are presented by broad region of birth, including Africa, Asia, Europe, Latin America and the Caribbean, Northern America, and Oceania. More detail is shown for Latin America and the Caribbean—including Mexico, Other Central America, South America, and the Caribbean. For this report, the category Other Central America excludes Mexico but includes the remaining countries of Central America.

Data are shown for population (e.g., age, marital status, occupation) and household (e.g., size, type, income) characteristics. A household is a person or a group of people who occupy a housing unit as their current residence. College residence halls, military barracks, correctional facilities, and other group quarters are not included. A householder is usually the person, or one of the people, in whose name the home is owned, being bought, or rented. A family household

Table 1 Population by Nativity Status and Citizenship: 2010
(Numbers in thousands. Data based on sample. For information on confidentiality protection, sampling error, and definitions, see www.census.gov/acs/www/)

Nativity and citizenship	Population[1]	Margin of error[2] (±)	Percent	Margin of error[2] (±)
Total	309,350	(X)	100.0	(X)
Native	269,394	115	87.1	—
Foreign born	39,956	115	12.9	—
Naturalized citizen	17,476	82	5.6	—
Noncitizen	22,480	120	7.3	—

(X) Not applicable.
— Represents or rounds to zero.
[1] Population as of July 1, 2010.
[2] Data are based on a sample and are subject to sampling variability. A margin of error is a measure of an estimate's variability. The larger the margin of error in relation to the size of the estimates, the less reliable the estimate. When added to and subtracted from the estimate, the margin of error forms the 90 percent confidence interval.
Source: U.S. Census Bureau, American Community Survey, 2010.
出典:The U.S. Census. 2012. "The Foreign-Born Population in the United States: 2010." *American Community Survey Reports*: 2. Retrieved March 23, 2013 (http://www.census.gov/prod/2012pubs/acs-19.pdf).

consists of a householder and one or more people living together in the same household who are related to the householder by birth, marriage, or adoption. It may also include people unrelated to the householder. The nativity status and place of birth of a household are determined by the nativity status and place of birth of the householder. A household with a foreign-born householder may also contain native residents, and a household with a native householder may also contain foreign-born residents.

The 2010 ACS estimated the number of foreign born in the United States to be nearly 40 million, or 13 percent of the total population (Table 1).

The foreign-born population from Latin America was the largest region-of-birth group, accounting for over half (53 percent) of all foreign born (Table 2).

Table 2 Foreign-Born Population by Region of Birth: 2010
(Numbers in thousands. Data based on sample. For information on confidentiality protection, sampling error, and definitions, see www.census.gov/acs/www/)

Region of birth	Population	Margin of error[1] (±)	Percent	Margin of error[1] (±)
Total[2]	39,956	115	100.0	(X)
Africa	1,607	33	4.0	0.1
Asia	11,284	47	28.2	0.1
Europe	4,817	44	12.1	0.1
Latin America and the Caribbean	21,224	90	53.1	0.1
Mexico	11,711	83	29.3	0.2
Other Central America	3,053	46	7.6	0.1
South America	2,730	42	6.8	0.1
Caribbean	3,731	42	9.3	0.1
Northern America	807	16	2.0	—
Oceania	217	10	0.5	—

(X) Not applicable.
— Represents or rounds to zero.
[1] Data are based on a sample and are subject to sampling variability. A margin of error is a measure of an estimate's variability. The larger the margin of error in relation to the size of the estimates, the less reliable the estimate. When added to and subtracted from the estimate, the margin of error forms the 90 percent confidence interval.
[2] Excludes 181 persons who reported they were born at sea.
Note: Percentages do not sum to 100.0 due to rounding.
Source: U.S. Census Bureau, American Community Survey, 2010.
出典：The U.S. Census. 2012. "The Foreign-Born Population in the United States: 2010." *American Community Survey Reports*: 2. Retrieved March 23, 2013 (http://www.census.gov/prod/2012pubs/acs-19.pdf).

By comparison, 28 percent of the foreign born were born in Asia, 12 percent in Europe, 4 percent in Africa, 2 percent in Northern America, and less than 1 percent in Oceania. Among the 21.2 million foreign born from Latin America, 11.7 million, or over half (55 percent), were born in Mexico. Of the total foreign-born population, 29 percent were born in Mexico.

Geographic Distribution

While the foreign born resided in every state in 2010, over half lived in just four states: California, New York, Texas, and Florida. Over one-fourth of the total foreign-born population lived in California. California, New York, and New Jersey had the highest foreign-born proportions in their total populations. Over 1 in 4 residents of California and over 1 in 5 residents of New York and New Jersey were foreign born.

Age, Marital Status, Fertility, and Household Size and Type

Half of the foreign born were between the ages of 18 and 44, compared with about one-third of the native born. The foreign born were also more likely than natives to be married and less likely to be divorced. Foreign-born households were, on average, larger than native households and were more likely to be family households, to include children under 18, and to be multigenerational. Foreign-born women were more likely to have given birth in the last 12 months than native women.

Year of Entry, Naturalization Rate, and English-Speaking Ability

Over half of the foreign born came to live in the United States since 1990, with about one-third entering the country in 2000 or later. Overall, about 2 in 5 foreign born were naturalized citizens. For those foreign born who entered before 1980, about 4 of 5 were naturalized citizens. About half of all foreign born either spoke only English at home or spoke a language other than English at home and spoke English "very well."

Educational Attainment, Labor Force Participation, and Occupation

Compared with the native-born population, the foreign born were less likely to be high school graduates. However, over 2 in 3 foreign born were high school graduates and more than 1 in 4 aged 25 years and older attained at least a bachelor's degree. The foreign born were more likely than the native born to be in the labor force. Over one-fourth of the foreign born worked in management, business, science, and art occupations with an additional one-fourth working in service occupations.

Household Income, Health Insurance Coverage, and Percent in Poverty

About two-thirds of the foreign born had some form of health insurance coverage and, of those, three-fourths were covered by a private insurer. The median income of foreign-born households was less than that of native households, and the foreign born were more likely than the native born to live in poverty. (840 words)

参考文献

The U.S. Census. 2012. "The Foreign-Born Population in the United States: 2010." *American Community Survey Reports*. Retrieved March 23, 2013 (http://www.census.gov/prod/2012pubs/acs-19.pdf).

用語解説

American Community Survey (ACS)　アメリカ・コミュニティ調査：アメリカに在住している人びとを対象に，アメリカ国勢調査局が毎年行っている調査．年齢，性別，人種，家族構成，収入，保険，教育，兵役経験，障害，住居と職に関する質問から構成されています．連邦政府・州政府が各コミュニティへの助成金の配分を決定する上で重要な指標となります．

labor force　労働力，労働人口：労働力とは，民間労働人口（civilian labor force）とアメリカ合衆国軍（陸軍，空軍，海軍，海兵隊，沿岸警備隊）で働く人びとを指します．民間労働人

口には，アメリカに在住する 16 歳以上の民間人のうち，「職に就いている人」と「働く意思があり，職を探しているが，職に就けていない人」が含まれています．

margin of error　誤差の範囲，許容誤差：信頼区間（confidence interval）の範囲．信頼区間とは，同一母集団から標本を何度も取り出した場合，母数の値 θ が含まれる標本を取り出せる確率を含む領域を指します．もし 95% 信頼区間に設定するのであれば，母数の値 θ を含む標本を取り出せる確率は 95% で，取り出せない確率が 5% となります．つまり，許容誤差は ± 5% です．詳しくは『統計学入門』（東京大学出版会，1991 年）を参照．

median income　平均収入：平均収入と和訳されている場合がありますが，実際は「収入の中央値（真ん中の値）」を指しています．収入の代表値を算出する場合，平均値（average）を計算すると，一部の富裕層などの外れ値（outliers）が，全体の平均値を押し上げるので中央値を用いています（図 4-1 を参照）．

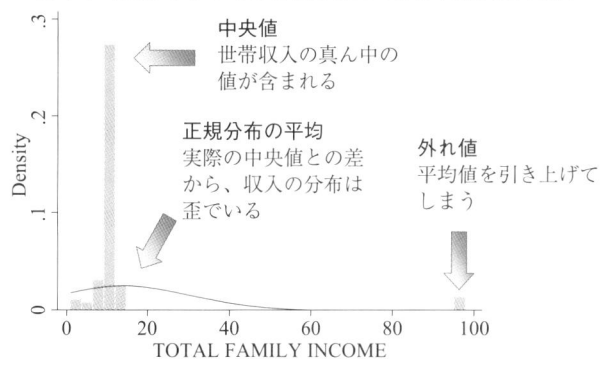

図 4-1　2008 年 アメリカの世帯収入でみる中央値と外れ値

出典：2008 年総合的社会調査（General Social Survey）より世帯収入（income）を用いて作成．

multigenerational　多世代：1 つ屋根の下に 3 世代以上が同居していること．例えば (1) 世帯主，世帯主の親，世帯主の子供，(2) 世帯主，世帯主の子供，世帯主の孫，(3) 世帯主，世帯主の両親と義父母，世帯主の子供，世帯主の孫，など．アメリカ国内の多世代家族に関する報告は，"Multigenerational Households: 2009 – 2011"（http://www.census.gov/prod/2012pubs/acsbr11-03.pdf）を参照．

問題 1．「外国生まれ」と「生粋」の違いを日本語で述べなさい．

問題 2．(1) 地理的分布 (2) 学歴と職業 (3) 世帯規模と健康保険加入状況ごとに，日本語で「外国生まれ」の特徴について述べなさい．

2. Analysis of General Hispanic Responses in the U.S. Census 2000

アメリカ国勢調査票には，回答者の人種・エスニシティを聞く項目があります．人種・エスニシティに関する情報は，各種団体への助成金を決定する上で重要な指標となります．正確な数値を得るために，アメリカ国勢調査局では，さまざまな取組が行われてきました．1990年までの国勢調査では，回答者は人種・エスニシティを1つしか選択できませんでしたが，2000年以降の国勢調査では，回答者は人種・エスニシティを複数選択することができるようになりました．調査票の質問と選択肢の文言を変えることで，人種・エスニシティ別の人口数に変化が生じるのでしょうか？ 1990年と2000年のデータを比較することで，ヒスパニック系人口の変容について学びましょう．

Prior to 1970, Hispanic origin was determined only indirectly. For example, the 1950 and 1960 censuses collected and published data for "persons of Spanish surname" in Arizona, California, Colorado, New Mexico, and Texas, whereas the 1940 census identified people who reported Spanish as their "mother tongue." Mexican was included as a category within the race question only in the 1930 census.

Although the 1970, 1980, 1990, and 2000 censuses all allowed self identification of Hispanic ethnicity, the actual question wording differed from one census to the next (see Figure 1).

The 1970 question was embedded within a question on place of birth on the 5-percent sample form and was worded: "Is this person's origin or descent - (fill one circle)." The 1970 census was the first to include a separate question specifically on Hispanic origin that was included on the 5-percent sample questionnaire. A similar question was first asked of everyone in 1980. Like the 1980 census, the 1970 census question allowed identification as "Mexican," "Puerto Rican," "Cuban," and "Other Spanish" categories, but the 1970 census included

第 4 章　アメリカ移民の現状 ── ヒスパニック系を事例に ──　77

Figure 1　Evolution of the Hispanic Question from the 1970 Census to the 2000 Census

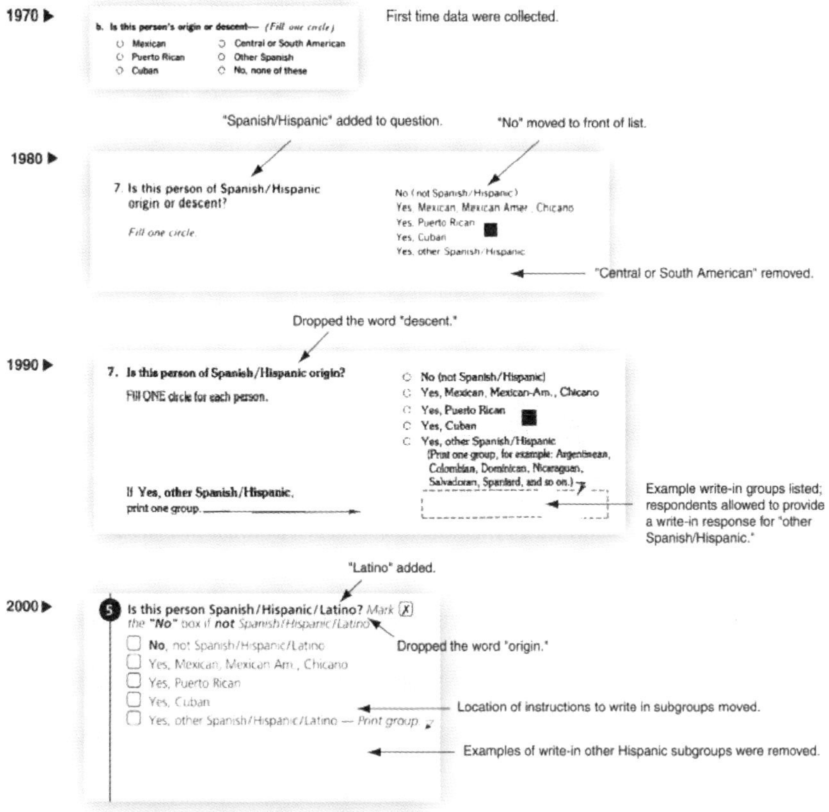

Source: U.S. Census Bureau.
出典：Cresce, Arthur R. and Roberto R. Ramirez. 2003. "Analysis of General Hispanic Responses in Census 2000." *Population Division Working Paper Series* No 72: 12. Retrieved March 23, 2013 (http://www.census.gov.edgekey.net/population/www/documentation/twps0072/twps0072.pdf

an additional category for "Central or South American" that did not appear in the 1980 question.

The 1980 question, asked on a 100-percent basis, was more direct in asking people to identify as Hispanic or not Hispanic and was worded, "Is this person of Spanish/Hispanic origin or descent?" The 1980 census provided response choices of "Mexican," "Puerto Rican," "Cuban," or "Other Spanish/Hispanic" origin but did not allow further identification of Hispanic ethnicity.

The 1990 census question ("Is ... of Spanish/Hispanic origin") was the same as the 1980 question except for the deletion of the words "or descent." The 1990 census was the only one to include examples of "other" Hispanic groups. In addition, this census was the first in which the groups that composed the "other Spanish/Hispanic" origin groups were coded and tabulated, although only for the portion of the population returning long forms.

The Census 2000 question was similar to the 1990 question except that the term "Latino" was added and the word "origin" was dropped ("Is this person Spanish/Hispanic/Latino?"). In Census 2000, people of Spanish/Hispanic/Latino origin could identify themselves as Mexican, Puerto Rican, Cuban, or other Spanish/Hispanic/Latino by marking a check box. People who marked "other Spanish/Hispanic/Latino" had additional space to write Hispanic origins, such as Salvadoran or Dominican, a practice started in the 1990 census. Unlike the 1990 census question, the Census 2000 question did not include examples of groups in the "other Spanish/Hispanic/Latino" category, but write-in responses were coded from all forms.

It is clear from this brief review that both question wording and format have changed with each census from 1970 to 2000. What is not clear is the impact these changes might have on the comparability of results among the censuses.

Table 1 shows the reported totals of Hispanic groups from the Census 2000 long form and the 1990 census sample (long) form.

All Hispanic groups increased between 1990 and 2000 except Nicaraguans, Uruguayans, and Spaniards. Spaniards, in particular, declined significantly. The largest proportionate increases occurred in the reporting of "Hispanic," "Latino," "Other Central American," and "Other South American." The latter two

Table 1 Hispanic Origin Population by Detailed Group: 2000 and 1990

Hispanic Population by Origin Response Number	1990 Census 2/ Number	Percent	Census 2000 2/ Number	Percent
Total	21,900,089	100	35,238,481	100
General Hispanic	1,403,150	6.4	5,540,627	15.7
Hispanic	390,945	1.8	2,316,515	6.6
Latino	1,577	0	411,559	1.2
Spanish	444,896	2	765,879	2.2
Other Hispanic response 1/	565,732	2.6	2,046,674	5.7
Mexican	13,393,208	61.2	20,900,102	59.3
Puerto Rican	2,651,815	12.1	3,403,510	9.7
Cuban	1,053,197	4.8	1,249,820	3.5
Dominican	520,151	2.4	799,768	2.3
Central American	1,323,830	6	1,811,676	5.3
Costa Rican	57,223	0.3	72,175	0.2
Guatemalan	268,779	1.2	407,127	1.2
Honduran	131,066	0.6	237,431	0.7
Nicaraguan	202,658	0.9	194,493	0.6
Panamanian	92,013	0.4	98,475	0.3
Salvadoran	565,081	2.6	708,741	2
Other Central American	7,010	0	93,234	0.1
South American	1,035,602	4.7	1,419,979	4
Argentinian	100,921	0.5	107,275	0.3
Bolivian	38,073	0.2	45,188	0.1
Chilean	68,799	0.3	73,951	0.2
Colombian	378,726	1.7	496,748	1.4
Ecuadorian	191,198	0.9	273,013	0.8
Paraguayan	6,662	0	8,929	0
Peruvian	175,035	0.8	247,601	0.7
Uruguayan	21,996	0.1	20,242	0.1
Venezuelan	47,997	0.2	96,091	0.3
Other South American	6,195	0	50,941	0.1
Spaniard	519,136	2.4	112,999	0.3

1/ Includes: (1) people who wrote responses such as "Latin American" and "Spanish American," (2) people of mixed Hispanic ethnicities (only collected in Census 2000), and (3) people who checked the "Other" box but did not provide a write-in entry

2/ These Census 2000 and 1990 census numbers are based on sample data representing the total population.

出典：Cresce, Arthur R. and Roberto R. Ramirez. 2003. "Analysis of General Hispanic Responses in Census 2000." *Population Division Working Paper Series* No 72: 3. Retrieved March 23, 2013 (http://www.census.gov.edgekey.net/population/www/documentation/twps0072/twps0072.pdf).

categories include specific write-in responses of "Central American" and "South American."

A different pattern emerges, however, when we look at the percent distribution of the Hispanic population by group between 1990 and 2000. The percentages of general Hispanic groups were generally higher in 2000 than in 1990, but the percentages of specific origin groups were generally either at the same percentage or lower in 2000 than in 1990. For example, the proportion of the Hispanic population providing a specific origin was 84.1 percent in Census 2000 and 93.6 percent in the 1990 census. The Mexican origin population declined from 61.2 percent in 1990 to 59.3 percent in 2000; Puerto Rican origin declined from 12.1 percent to 9.7 percent; Cuban origin declined from 4.8 percent to 3.5 percent. The most dramatic decline was for reports of Spaniard, which fell from 2.4 percent to 0.3 percent.

Contrasting increases in the percentages of the general groups mirrored the declines in specific groups. For example, the percent "Latino" increased from less than 0.1 percent to 1.2 percent, "Hispanic" increased from 1.8 percent to 6.6 percent, "Spanish" increased slightly from 2.0 percent to 2.2 percent, and "Other Hispanic" increased from 2.6 percent to 5.8 percent. "Other Hispanic" includes: (1) people who provided responses such as "Latin American" and "Spanish American"; (2) people of mixed Hispanic ethnicities (only collected in Census 2000); and (3) people who checked the "Other" box but did not provide a write-in entry. Thus, it is clear that the differences in the percentage distribution by Hispanic group reflect a shift in the reported composition of the Hispanic population.(791words)

参考文献

Population Division Working Paper Series No 72. Retrieved March 23, 2013 (http://www.census.gov.edgekey.net/population/www/ documentation/twps0072/twps0072.pdf).

用語解説

census tract level　国勢統制区：アメリカ国勢調査用に細分化した区域を指します．人口密度の高い地域を，人口数（2,500人〜8,000人）や居住者の社会経済的地位などが均一になるように区分けすることで，時系列的に地域内に見られる変化を分析できるようにしています．詳しくは"Census Tracts and Block Numbering Areas" (www.census.gov/reference/pdfs/GARM/Ch10GARM.pdf)を参照．

ethnicity　エスニシティ，人種（race）との違いはp. 89を参照．：生活様式，宗教，習俗，言語などに共通が見られる共同体．「文化的違いの見られる社会組織（the social organization of cultural difference）」(Barth 1969) と「社会的違いの見られる文化組織（the cultural organization of social difference）」(Geertz 1973) の言葉に見られるように，今日ではエスニシティという概念を広義に捉えています．例えば，文化的に多様な集団であったとしても，同じエスニシティを共有している場合もありますし（ユダヤ系，ムスリム系，など），文化的類似性が見られたとしても，異なるエスニシティを持っている場合（中国人，台湾人など）もあります．エスニシティの境目は，時代の社会的文脈によって作られ，また他者との関係性をベースに変容します．

Spanish/Hispanic/Latino　スペイン系／ヒスパニック系／ラティーノ系：エスニシティに関する質問で使われる表現．スペイン系とは欧州を，ヒスパニック系とはスペイン語を話す地域を，ラティーノ系とは主に南米を出自とする人たちを指します．アメリカの国勢調査では，回答者自身が自分の人種・エスニシティを選択・記載する仕組みになっているため，個々人の主観に基づいたデータが集められています．

long forms　長い調査票：1940年から2000年の国勢調査で使用されていました．2010年国勢調査では使用廃止が決定し，代わりにアメリカン・コミュニティ調査を実施することが決定しました．長い調査票では，短い調査票で聞かれる項目（氏名，性別，年齢，続柄，人種，ヒスパニック系か否か，自宅保有の有無）に加えて，婚姻歴，出生地，国籍，祖先，入国年，学歴，収入，職場，通勤時間，住居環境，5年間前の居住地，自宅で使用する言語，兵役経験，障害の有無，祖父母が孫の面倒を見ているかなどの質問が含まれています．詳しくは"The Long and Short of It" (http://www.census.gov/dmd/www/pdf/d3239a.pdf)を参照．

問題1．人種・エスニシティに関する質問の文言が（1）1970年（2）1980年（3）1990年（4）2000年ごとに異なっています．それぞれを日本語で答えなさい．

問題2．1990年と2000年のヒスパニック系人口を比較すると，どのような特徴・違いが見られますか？日本語で述べなさい．

3. Demography of Hispanic Identity

アイデンティティーとは自分が何者であるかを自己の中で保持する概念です.これには,他者の眼差しによって決められる「相対的な要素」と,自分自身で決定する(希望的な側面も含めて)「絶対的な要素」が含まれています.「ヒスパニック系アメリカ人」と十把一絡げにされますが,その内訳を出身国,世代,経済力,教育レベルなどから改めて比較してみると,ヒスパニック系アイデンティティーに対する,個々人の認識の違いが見られます.ピュー・ヒスパニック・センター (Pew Hispanic Center) では,アメリカに在住するヒスパニック系を対象に独自の調査を行っています.ヒスパニック系移民やヒスパニック系アメリカ人のアイデンティティーについて学びましょう.

Latinos have many different ways to describe their identity—including pan-ethnic terms like "Hispanic" or "Latino," or the term "American," or terms that refer to their family's country of origin. Their choices vary among different Latino subgroups, with nativity and language usage the strongest predictors of identity preferences.

Terms Used Most Often to Describe Identity
Among first-generation (or immigrant) Hispanics, more than six-in-ten (62%) say they most often use their family's country of origin to describe themselves. Among second-generation Hispanics, the share using their family's country of origin falls to 43%. And among third-generation Hispanics, the share falls to just 28%—less than half that seen among immigrant Hispanics.

Not surprisingly, the use of the term "American" increases in a mirror-image pattern. While just 8% of immigrant Hispanics most often call themselves American, that share rises to 35% among second-generation Hispanics and 48% among third-generation Hispanics.

Use of the pan-ethnic terms "Hispanic" or "Latino" to describe identity also varies across generations, but the pattern is not as notable. Among immigrant Hispanics, 28% say they most often describe themselves as "Hispanic" or "Latino." Among second-generation Hispanics, this share falls to 18%; among those in the third generation, it's 21%.

Across other subgroups of Hispanics, the less educated and Spanish dominant are more likely than the more educated and English dominant to use their family's country of origin to describe their identity. More than six-in-ten Spanish- dominant Hispanics (63%) say they most often use the name of their family's country of origin to describe themselves, and nearly as many Hispanics with less than a high school diploma (57%) say the same. By contrast, just 37% of the native born and one-third (33%) of the English dominant say they call themselves by the names of their ancestral countries.

As noted earlier, use of the term "American" mirrors that of country of origin, in reverse. While Spanish-dominant Hispanics are most likely to say they call themselves by their family's country of origin most often, just 4% say they most often describe themselves as American. Among Hispanics who have less than a high school diploma, only 10% say they most often use the term American. Meanwhile, 40% of native-born Latinos and 48% of English-dominant Latinos say they most often describe themselves as American.

Hispanics and Racial Identification

When it comes to racial identification, many Hispanics' self-assessments do not fit into the racial classifications used by the U.S. Census Bureau and the federal government. Findings from the Pew Hispanic survey show that, when asked which term describes their race—white, black, Asian or some other race—51% of Latinos say their race is either "some other race" (26%) or volunteer that their race is "Hispanic or Latino" (25%). Meanwhile, one-third (36%) say their race is white and the remainder, 10%, identify their race as black, Asian or mixed race.

These findings do not match those of the 2010 U.S. Census. According to the U.S. Census Bureau, when asked about their race, 37% of all Latinos identified their race as "some other race" and more than half (53%) identified their race as white (Humes, Jones and Ramirez, 2011).

The Pew Hispanic survey also finds that racial identification among Latinos varies by immigrant generation, with third-generation Latinos the most likely to identify as white. Among immigrant Latinos, 52% say their race is "some other race" (21%) or "Hispanic or Latino" (31%), 36% say their race is white and 9% say their race is black, Asian or mixed race. Among second-generation Latinos, a similar pattern is evident—56% say their race is either "some other race" (36%) or "Hispanic or Latino" (20%), followed by 30% who say their race is white. Among third-generation Hispanics, the share that identifies as white rises to 44% and the share that says "some other race" or "Hispanic or Latino" falls to 43%.

A Typical American— Or Not?

When asked whether they see themselves as a "typical American," Hispanics are evenly split—47% say they are "a typical American" and another 47% say they are "very different" from a typical American. These responses vary sharply across demographic subgroups of Hispanics. Those who are more affluent, English dominant and U.S. born are most likely to call themselves a typical American. Among Hispanics who make more than $75,000 a year, 70% say they see themselves as a typical American. Among third-generation Hispanics, 69% say the same, as do two-thirds (66%) of English- dominant Hispanics and two-thirds of native-born Hispanics (66%).

By contrast, just 31% of Hispanics who are Spanish dominant, 34% of foreign-born Hispanics and 36% of Hispanics with less than a high school education say they are a typical American. Among these same three groups, majorities say they are "very different from the typical American."

Shared Hispanic Culture among U.S. Hispanics—Or Not?

By a margin of more than two-to-one across nearly all major demographic subgroups of Hispanics, more say U.S. Hispanics have many different cultures than say they share a common culture.

For example, among college-educated Hispanics, 74% say U.S. Hispanics have many different cultures, while just 25% say they share a common culture. Results are similar among the foreign born (71% versus 27%), the Spanish dominant (70% versus 28%) and Mexican- origin Hispanics (67% versus 30%). Even among those who are U.S. born with U.S.- born parents, nearly twice as many say U.S. Hispanics have many different cultures as say they share a common culture—62% versus 36%. (900 words)

参考文献
Taylor, Paul, Mark Hugo Lopez, Jessica Hamar Martinez and Gabriel Velasco. 2012. "When Labels Don't Fit: Hispanics and Their Views of Identity." Pew Hispanic Center. Retrieved March 23, 2013 (http://www.pewhispanic.org/files/2012/04/PHC-Hispanic-Identity.pdf).

用語解説
culture 文化：ある集団が共用する価値観．文化社会学では，文化を美術・芸術・文学という分野だけに限定しません．
pan-ethnicity 汎エスニシティ：複数のエスニシティを一つにまとめた呼び方の総称．アジア系，ヒスパニック系などが該当します．
race 人種：エスニシティとの違いはp. 85を参照．見た目の違いを根拠に作られた階層システム．近代化社会の産物として考えられていますが，旧約聖書の『ノアの箱船』の中で，黒人種のハムが白人種のセムの奴隷として仕えるようにと書かれていることから，人種差別の起源は聖書にあるのではないかとも考えられています．人種という概念は，それぞれの国によって異なります．アメリカ合衆国では，黒人の血が一滴でも入っている場合は黒人と見なすという考えがあり，これを「一滴規定（one-drop rule）」と言います．1910年，一滴規定が初めて法律としてテネシー州とルイジアナ州で明文化されました．

問題 1. 本文を読んで，「ヒスパニック系にみる世代別アイデンティティー」と

いう表を作成しなさい．
問題2．「自分は典型的なアメリカ人」であると答える傾向の高いヒスパニック系の特徴を日本語で述べなさい．

4．Deportation Relief for Unauthorized Immigrants Youth

不法移民の子供には，幼少の頃に親と共にアメリカへ不法入国した人たちと，アメリカ国内で不法滞在者の両親から産まれた人たちとがいます．アメリカでは，不法滞在をしている子供たちにも無償で初等・中等教育を受けることが認められています．高校卒業後に大学へ進学する人たちもいますが，正規ビザがないために，大学卒業後に定職に就くことが容易ではありません．オバマ大統領はこのような若者らに永住権を与える「ドーリム・アクト（Dream Act）」という法案の成立を目指してきましたが，議会で承認されませんでした．そこで議会の承認を必要としない大統領覚書（presidential memorandum）で，2012年6月に児童期入国移民在留合法化プログラム（Deferred Action for Childhood Arrivals）を導入しました．そして大統領選挙を目前とした2012年8月15日から受付を開始しました．ここでは，児童期入国移民在留合法化プログラムについて学びましょう．

Updated Eligibility Guidelines

On August 3, 2012, the Department of Homeland Security published updated eligibility guidelines for the Deferred Action for Childhood Arrivals program.

According to the updated guidelines, unauthorized immigrants ages 15 to 30 who arrived in the U.S. before age 16 may qualify for deferred action if:

- They have continuously resided in the U.S. since June 15, 2007;
- They have physically present in the U.S. on June 15, 2012;
- They are enrolled in school, have a high school diploma or a GED, or have been honorably discharged from the military or Coast Guard by the time of

their application;

- And they have not been convicted of a felony, a significant misdemeanor offense, or three or more other misdemeanors, and do not present a threat to national security or public safety.

Unauthorized immigrants who meet these criteria may apply for a deferred action permit that shields them from deportation for two years and also may potentially qualify them for work authorization. At the expiration of the two-year deferred action period, program beneficiaries can apply for a two-year renewal, pending a review of their case. According to DHS, renewals will be issued in two-year increments. Unauthorized immigrants who are currently in removal proceedings or have a removal order also may apply for deferred action if they meet the eligibility guidelines set by DHS.

As DHS has noted, this new program does not provide a path to permanent resident status or citizenship. Also, immediate relatives or dependents of potential beneficiaries cannot be considered for deferred action.

The DHS, through U.S. Citizenship and Immigration Services (USCIS), will begin accepting applications from unauthorized immigrants ages 15 to 30 on August 15, 2012. According to USCIS, each deferred action request will be evaluated on a case-by-case basis. A $465 application fee applies to each request and includes fees for the deferred action permit and fees for a temporary work authorization permit.

How Many Potentially Eligible Now

The Pew Hispanic analysis finds that among the 1.7 million unauthorized immigrants ages 30 and under who are potentially eligible to participate in the deferred action program, some 950,000 may be immediately eligible. This includes 700,000 unauthorized immigrants ages 15 to 17 who are currently enrolled in school. Young unauthorized immigrants who may be immediately eligible make up more than half (55%) of the 1.7 million potential beneficiaries of the new program.

The Pew Hispanic estimates shown in this report do not take into account young unauthorized immigrants who may be potential beneficiaries through military or Coast Guard service rather than educational attainment – likely a small number of potential beneficiaries. Honorably discharged veterans who meet age and residency criteria qualify to take part in the deferred action program.

The Pew Hispanic estimates also do not take into account felony or misdemeanor status. Those who have been convicted of a felony, a significant misdemeanor or three or more misdemeanors are not eligible to participate in the deferred action program.

How Many Not Eligible Now, But May Be in the Future

Applying the updated eligibility guidelines recently published by DHS, the Pew Hispanic analysis finds that there are 770,000 young unauthorized immigrants who are not currently eligible for deferred action, but may become eligible in the future. This includes 450,000 unauthorized immigrants under age 15 who are currently enrolled in school and have been in the U.S. continuously for at least five years. They would eventually age into program eligibility.

As noted earlier, an additional 320,000 unauthorized immigrants ages 16 to 30 who arrived in the U.S. as children and have been continuously in the U.S. for at least five years, but do not have a high school diploma of GED, could be eligible. Unauthorized immigrants in this group would become potentially eligible if they enrolled in school before applying for deferred deportation action. School enrollment is a key condition of DHS' unpublished eligibility guidelines.

Ineligible Unauthorized Immigrants

Not all unauthorized immigrants ages 30 and under are eligible for deferred deportation action under the new program. According to the Pew Hispanic analysis, some 2.4 million meet the age requirements of the administration's program but arrived in the U.S. after age 15 or have been here less than five years, making them ineligible. An additional 280,000 unauthorized immigrants who are under age 15 are also not eligible for the deferred action policy since they have not been in the U.S. for five years ore more, the cutoff residency requirement of the program.

The deferred action policy also excludes any unauthorized immigrant childhood arrivals who arrive in the U.S. after June 15, 2012. These new arrivals do not qualify for deferred action and, unlike some potentially eligible young unauthorized immigrants, cannot age into eligibility. There are estimated 11.2 million unauthorized immigrants in the U.S., according to estimates from the Pew Hispanic Center (Passel and Cohn, 2011). As previously noted, they include 4.4 million who are ages 30 and under. An additional 6.8 million unauthorized immigrants ages 31 and older, who make up more than 60% of the nation's 11.2 million unauthorized immigrants, are not addressed by the deferred action program.

参考文献
Passel, Jeffery S and Mark Hugo Lopez. 2012. "Up to 1.7 Million Unauthorized Immigrant Youth May Benefit from New Deportation Rules." Pew Hispanic Center. Retrieved Marcy 23, 2013 http://www.pewhispanic.org/files/2012/unauthorized_immigrant_youth_update.pdf).

用語解説
GED (General Education Development) certificate　総合教育開発証書：アメリカまたはカナダの高校卒業程度の学力があることを証明する証書．英語ライティング，英語読解，社会，科学，数学の5教科から構成されています．
honorably discharged veterans　名誉除隊者：与えられた任務を遂行し，「非常に良い」か「良い」という評価を得られれば，名誉除隊の称号が与えられます．アメリカ政府は，合法移民・不法移民にかかわらず，アメリカ国内に在住する18歳から25歳の男性に対して選抜徴兵制度（Selective Service System）に登録することを法律で義務づけています．そのため不法移

民であったとしても，アメリカ合衆国軍に徴兵される可能性はあります．アメリカ合衆国国土安全保障省（U.S. Department of Homeland Security）が法令の中に名誉除隊者について触れていることから，実際に不法滞在者がアメリカ合衆国軍に入隊していることがわかります．

U.S. Citizenship and Immigration Services　アメリカ市民権・移民業務局：アメリカ合衆国国土安全保障省の下に設けられた連邦政府組織．2001年にアメリカ同時多発テロ事件が起こった後，当時大統領であったジョージ・W・ブッシュ氏は移民帰化局（Immigration and Naturalization Services）をアメリカ司法省から国土安全保障省へ移すことで，新たに入国する外国人とアメリカ国内に滞在する外国人に対しての取締を強化しました．

問題1　児童期入国移民在留合法化プログラムの申請する際の条件を日本語で述べなさい．

問題2　ピュー・ヒスパニック・センターの調査によると，30歳以下であったとしても，児童期入国移民在留合法化プログラムに申請する資格がない人たちもいます．非該当者について，日本語で述べなさい．

解　答

1. Foreign-born Populations in the United States – 2010

問題1　「外国生まれ（foreign born）」とはアメリカ国外で出生した人で，この中には帰化アメリカ人，永住権保持者，一時移民（学生など），難民，不法移民を含みます．それに対して「生粋（native born）」とは，アメリカ合衆国，プエルトリコ，米国諸島で産まれた人を指します．アメリカ国外で生まれたとしても，両親のうち1人でもアメリカ国籍であれば「生粋」に含まれます．

問題2　(1) 外国生まれの人たちの半数以上は，カリフォルニア州，ニューヨーク州，テキサス州，フロリダ州のいずれかに住んでいます．(2) 高校卒業程度の学歴のある外国生まれの人たちは，3人中2人です．25歳以上の外国生まれのうち，大学卒業程度の学歴があるひとたちは4人中1人です．外国生まれの人たちの1/4は管理職，事業，科学，芸術の分野で働いています．さらに1/4の人たちはサービス業で働いています．(3) 外国生まれの世帯には18歳以下の子供がいて，多世代世帯である場合が多いです．外国生まれの人たちの2/3は，健康保険に加入しており，そのうち3/4の人たちは民間の健康保険に加入しています．

2. Analysis of General Hispanic Responses in the U.S. Census 2000

問題1 (1) 質問は「この人の生まれ (origin), または祖先は (descent)」. 回答は「メキシコ人, プエルトリコ人, キューバ人, 中央・南アメリカ人, その他スペイン人, 該当なし」の6択. 全員ではなく5%サンプルにだけ質問票を配布. (2) 質問は「この人の生まれ, または祖先はスペイン系／ヒスパニック系ですか」. 回答は「いいえ, はい メキシコ人・メキシコ系アメリカ人・チカノ, はい プエルトリコ人, はい キューバ人, はい その他スペイン系／ヒスパニック系」の5択. 質問票は全員に配布. (3) 1980年の質問と基本的に同じ内容ですが「祖先」を削除しました. 選択肢も同じ内容ですが「その他スペイン系／ヒスパニック系」を選択した人は自由回答することが可能となりました. ただし, 1つだけ書くようにとの指示がありました. 全員ではなく長い調査票を受取った人だけが対象です. (4) 1990年の質問と基本的に同じ内容ですが「ラティーノ」が追加され「生まれ」を削除しました. 選択肢も基本的に同じ内容ですが, 自由記述欄の指示文を削除しました.

問題2 1990年と2000年を比べると, ニカラグア人, ウルグアイ人, スペイン人以外のヒスパニック系は増加しています. 割合別にみてみると, ヒスパニック系一般は増加していますが (6.4% → 15.7%), エスニシティを1つだけ挙げている人たちの割合は減少しています (メキシコ人 61.2% → 59.3%, プエルトリコ人 12.1% → 9.7%, キューバ人 4.8% → 3.5%, スペイン人 2.4% → 0.3%).

3. Demography of Hispanic Identity

問題1

表 4-1 ヒスパニック系にみるアイデンティティー

	出身国	ヒスパニック系／ラティーノ系	アメリカ人
第1世代	62%	28%	8%
第2世代	43%	18%	35%
第3世代	28%	21%	48%

問題2 自分が典型的なアメリカ人だと考えるヒスパニック系の特徴は, 裕福, 英語が第1言語, アメリカ生まれ. 個別に見てみると (1) 年間所得が7万5,000ドル以上の人たちのうち70% (2) 第1言語が英語である人たちのうち66% (3) 第3世代のうち69% (4) アメリカ生まれのうち66% という特徴があります.

4. Deportation Relief for Unauthorized Immigrants Youth

問題1　現在15歳から30歳までの不法移民で，アメリカ入国が16歳以前である者が対象．そして（1）2007年6月15日以降からアメリカに継続して在住していること（2）2012年6月15日以降，アメリカ国外に出国していないこと（3）就学していること，または高校卒業証書か総合教育開発証書（GED）があること，あるいは軍隊か沿岸警備隊から名誉除隊していること（4）重罪・軽犯罪を犯していないこと，アメリカの安全保障や公衆安全を脅かす存在でないこと．

問題2　（1）年齢枠にあてはまらない人たち．14歳以下または31歳以上は該当しません．（2）該当年齢であったとしても在住期間が5年に満たない人たちもいます．（3）2007年6月15日以降に不法入国した人たちは対象外．超過滞在者であれば入国日を証明することは簡単ですが，不法入国者の場合は他の書類で証明する必要が生じます．

第5章

アメリカ大統領制と大統領のレトリック

はじめに

第5章では，アメリカ大統領制と大統領のレトリックがどのように発展したのかを解説する．解説に加えてそうした発展の中で要となった演説の原文を読むことで理解を深める．また理解度を確認するための設問を付した．

1. 大統領制の起源と建国初期

In the Constitutional Convention, the specific issues of executive design included the number of executive, the method of executive selection and succession, the length and character of the term of office, the means of removal in extraordinary circumstances, and the enumerated powers of the executive. The executive should be unitary. The convention proposed the electoral college as a method to elect the president, with no restriction on the reelection. The president would be selected by a majority vote of the electors, who would be chosen by the sates using whatever methods each states adopted. The convention's recommendation was that electoral college choose the president for a four-year term. The delegates realized they should provide for situation in which the executive had to be removed from office before the term expired. Serious abuse of power was one such situation, and the remedy was impeachment. The president had the enumerated powers—that is, a veto, a right to direct the armed forces as commander in chief, a right to require the opinion of the principal officer in each of the executive departments, a pardon power, a power of making all treaties with approbation and advice of the Senate, an appointment power with Senate confirmation, a duty to give information to the legislature of the state of the Union, a right to convene the House and Senate on extraordinary occasions, a power to receive ambassadors, and a general authority to execute the federal laws.

On April 30, 1789, George Washington made the first inaugural. The presidential inaugural address is a discourse whose significance all recognize. They are an essential element in a ritual of transition in which the covenant between the citizenry and their leaders is renewed.

Washington considered the heads of every Cabinet and department to be his deputies and exerted full authority over the executive branch, having the final say in major and minor decisions. Congressional opponents of a strong presidency attempted to limit the executive's removal of chief Cabinet officers, but Congress soon validated the president's power to replace Cabinet heads in the so-called Decision of 1789.

Washington considered the separation of powers crucial. Following a discomfiting visit to the Senate to discuss a treaty, he decided that all future communications with Congress would take place through written correspondence. In April 1792, Washington issued the first veto. Through his reports to Congress and his first veto, Washington put in motion the operation of the checks and balances that continues to exist between the executive and legislative branches.

Despite his efforts to avoid criticism, resistance to presidential authority erupted over Washington's divisive policies. At the end of his second term Washington published a Farewell Address warning against a foreign alliance, domestic factions and party politics.

Farewell Address, September 17, 1796.

The great rule of conduct for us in regard to foreign nations is in extending our commercial relations, to have with them as little political connection as possible. So far as we have already formed engagements, let them be fulfilled with perfect good faith. Here let us stop. Europe has a set of primary interests which to us have none; or a very remote relation. Hence she must be engaged in frequent controversies, the causes of which are essentially foreign to our concerns. Hence, therefore, it must be unwise in us to implicate ourselves by artificial ties in the ordinary vicissitudes of her politics, or the ordinary combinations and collisions of her friendships or enmities.

設問 1. 大統領はどのように選ばれるか.
設問 2. 1789 年の決定とは何か.
設問 3. 告別の辞でワシントンは何を主張しているか.

2. ジェファソン・デモクラシー期から南北戦争

Thomas Jefferson immediately discontinued what he perceived as elitist and monarchial patterns of behavior. To reduce the pomp and ceremony of the presidency, he chose to send written the State of Union addresses. From that time until Woodrow Wilson reinstated oral delivery, the State of Union addresses were written.

Jefferson broadened presidential powers further when he purchased Louisiana from France in 1803. The greatest expansion of presidential powers during Jefferson's presidency came during the embargo of 1807-1809. Democratic-Republican controlled Congress placed state militias under presidential control to circumvent uncooperative Federalist governors, and the president could intervene in court cases involving enforcement.

On the War of 1812, Critics generally target James Madison's record as a wartime president and label him a failure. Indeed, regardless of his belief in a strong executive, by temperament and personality Madison was ill-suited for the demands placed on a wartime president. But Madison did not acquiesce to House Democratic-Republicans' calls for a sedition law to suppress antiwar protests. Nor did he dignify the Federalist's Hartford Convention demands for constitutional amendments to curtail the power of the presidency.

James Monroe ushered in a new era in presidential diplomacy when he issued the Monroe Doctrine, warning Europe against intervention and colonization in the Americas. With the Federalist Party in rapid decline, Monroe presided over a period of decreased partisanship dubbed the "Era of Good Feelings."

Noting that the presidency was the only federal office elected by all of the American people, Andrew Jackson on that basis pushed the presidency to its constitutional limits. The claim had validity, because by 1832 presidential electors were chosen by popular vote in every state but South Carolina. Jackson transformed the presidency into an office held by the direct representative of the people who claimed an electoral mandate. During his eight years in office, Jackson reshaped the contours of the presidency and established new boundaries of presidential power through his spoils system, his effort to destroy the Bank of the United States. Most of the presidents who came after Jackson pursed a tradition laid down by him.

Deeming national expansion as the last hope for preserving the Union, Franklin Pierce and James Buchanan emphasized the idea of manifest destiny to expand westward. When South Carolina seceded in December 1860, Buchanan claimed that a strict construction of the president's constitutional powers limited his ability to respond to the crisis. Despite the many problems with a strict functional separation of powers, many presidents in the nineteenth century followed Buchanan in this approach to the office.

Abraham Lincoln took a completely different approach to constitutional interpretation. He justified a broad interpretation of the executive power and the commander in chief clause throughout the Civil War. The attack on federal troops at Fort Sumter occurred while Congress in recess. Nearly simultaneously, mobs in Baltimore were blocking the passage of troops en route to guard the capital.

Lincoln was thus forced to act. Within days, he called out the militia to protect Washington. He then suspended the writ of habeas corpus in Maryland, blockaded Southern ports, and sent weapons to loyalists. He justified invoking his authority as commander in chief without a declaration of war by Congress.

Lincoln is arguably the greatest of all presidents. This is not because of how he expanded the powers of the presidency but because of the prudence and conscience with which he used them. The Gettysburg Address described a country dedicated to a new birth of freedom by the reinstatement of the declaration of the Independence. The freedom reborn was of a qualitatively different kind than what had existed previously.

Gettysburg Address, November 19, 1863.

Four score and seven years ago our fathers brought forth on this continent a new nation, conceived in liberty, and dedicated to the proposition that all men are created equal...

It is for us the living, rather, to be dedicated here to the unfinished work which they who fought here have thus far so nobly advanced. It is rather for us to be here dedicated to the great task remaining before us—that from these honored dead we take increased devotion to that cause for which they gave the last full measure of devotion—that we here highly resolve that these dead shall not have died in vain—that this nation, under God, shall have a new birth of freedom and that government of the people, by the people, for the people, shall not perish from the earth.

設問1. ジェファソンはどのような行動をとることで大統領の権限を拡大したか.
設問2. ジャクソン政権期における大統領制の大きな変化は何か.
設問3. リンカンはどのような戦争権限を行使したのか.

設問 4. ゲティスバーグ演説の意義は何か.

3. 南北戦争から革新主義の時代

After Lincoln's assassination, Andrew Johnson battled with Congress over the direction of Reconstruction policy. Congress was motivated to impeach Johnson for his obstruction of Reconstruction legislation. In the end, the Republicans failed to get a two-thirds majority for conviction. The power and stature of the presidency declined after Jackson, peaked at the death of Lincoln, and receded rapidly thereafter.

The election of Ulysses S. Grant in 1868 didn't revive the power of the executive. If the American people thought they were electing a forceful leader in Grant, they ware sorely mistaken. Lacking experience in civil administration, Grant had neither the detailed knowledge of the government process needed to perform the role of chief executive nor the political experience needed to bend other leaders to his purposes. While Johnson fought Congress and lost, Grant appeared to surrender without a fight.

Grant left the office he had occupied for eight years at a low ebb. The Senate, its leader believed, was secure in its mastery over the executive. Yet Rutherford B. Hayes was determined to emancipate the executive from congressional domination. During the Hayes administration, the powers of the presidency were defended persistently and effectively for the first time since the Civil War.

The assassination of James A. Garfield had enflamed public opinion against the spoils system, and Chester A. Arthur quickly realized that if he did not support civil service reform, he would jeopardize the dominant political position. The president called on Congress to pass the Pendleton Act.

The civil service reform bill contained measures, such as competitive examinations for federal jobs and a ban on political assessments. The enactment of civil service reform in 1883 was a fundamental turning point in the history of the federal administrative system.

By 1889 the post-Civil War decline in the prestige of the presidency came to an end. The Senate's grip on the details of administration, especially the removal power, was loosened by the defeats administered by Hayes, Garfield, and Grover Cleveland. The struggle to rejuvenate executive independence was advanced by the enactment of civil service reform, which began the process of insulating federal appointments from the parochial concerns of party spoilsmen.

William McKinley's tenure marked an important transformation of the presidency. McKinley's legislative leadership was active. Indeed, he was the first post-Civil War president to take the political initiative in Washington without arousing the resentment of his party in Congress. Furthermore the acquisition of the Philippines broadened the international obligations of the United States. Congress authorized the executive to create a military government in the Philippines. Thus did McKinley, a wartime president, capitalize on a foreign crisis and it is aftermath to expand the powers of the presidency beyond the limits that had constrained his predecessors.

During the last three decades of the nineteenth century, major changes in American society placed greater burdens on the national government, and particularly on the presidency. The population of the United States doubled between 1870 and 1900. Urbanization and immigration increased at extraordinary rates. These changes were accompanied by a shift in business activity to the mammoth national corporations. The greater concentration of wealth at the turn of the century yielded giant trusts that constituted uncontrolled and irresponsible bastions of power. These combinations aroused fears that growing corporate influence might jeopardize the equal opportunity of individuals to climb the economic ladder. Moreover, many people believed that the great business interests had captured and corrupted the men and methods of government for their own profit.

The protest against the financial exploitation and political corruption that industrial growth unleashed was the progressive movement. Because progressivism represented the fastest-growing segments of the population, it had a major influence on the nation. Furthermore the progressive movement helped foster important changes in the presidency. Although the executive office had developed significantly in the hands of strong leaders, most of the powers of the president remained tightly restricted until the twentieth century. Congressional government was the prevailing theme of late nineteenth-century politics in America.

Theodore Roosevelt changed the old pattern. Roosevelt proclaimed that the president is "a steward of the people." Dedicated to the progressive concept of active, executive-centered government, he advocated and practiced a vigorous form of leadership that broadly extended the reach of presidential influence. But Roosevelt was no enemy to business or party interests. He accepted the new industrial order, wanting only to curb its worst excess through government regulation. He described belief in the inaugural address as follows.

Inaugural Address, March 4, 1905.

Our relations with the other powers of the world are important; but still more important are our relations among ourselves. Such growth in wealth, in population, and in power as this nation has seen during the century and a quarter of its national life is inevitably accompanied by a like growth in the problems which are ever before every nation that rises to greatness. Power invariably means both responsibility and danger. Our forefathers faced certain perils which we have outgrown. We now face other perils, the very existence of which it was impossible that they should foresee. Modern life is both complex and intense, and the tremendous changes wrought by the extraordinary industrial development of the last half century are felt in every fiber of our social and political being. Never before have men tried so vast and formidable an experiment as that of administering the affairs of a continent under the forms of a democratic republic. The conditions which have told for our marvelous material well-being, which have developed to a very high degree our energy, self-reliance, and individual initiative, have also brought the care and anxiety inseparable from the accumulation of great wealth in industrial centers. Upon the success of our experiment much depends, not only as regards our own welfare, but as regards the welfare of mankind. If we fail, the cause of free self-government throughout the world will rock to its foundations, and therefore our responsibility is heavy, to ourselves, to the world as it is today, and to the generations yet unborn.

Roosevelt's determination to use the presidency to serve the public interest, as he understood it, brought about a number of significant changes in the conduct of the executive office. Arguably, the most important of these changes was to advance the president's role as the leader of public opinion. Roosevelt ushered in the "rhetorical presidency"—that is, the use of popular rhetoric as a principal technique of presidential leadership.

The rise of the rhetorical presidency signified a dramatic transformation of the founding constitutional theory and early history of the presidency. The framers of the Constitution had wanted to proscribe popular presidential leadership. During the nineteenth century efforts by the president to rouse the public to support him or his policies were considered illegitimate, a form of demagogy that was beneath the dignity of the office. Roosevelt's "stewardship" theory of the executive, however, required the president to forge more personal ties with the public. Accordingly, at times Roosevelt appealed directly to the people to bring pressure to bear on members of Congress who were reluctant to support his policies.

Roosevelt's innovative and pathbreaking activism in domestic affairs, important as it was, pales by comparison with his conduct of foreign policy. In foreign affairs, he believed that new conditions dictated a more decisive break with the past. Although the president's authority to initiate foreign policy and to negotiate treaties had become settled practice during the nineteenth century, Roosevelt also asserted primacy in the execution of such matters, even when congressional support was lacking.

設問1. ペンドルトン法とはどのような法律か.
設問2. 革新主義はどのような背景で生まれたのか.
設問3. ローズヴェルトは大企業の専横に対してどのような姿勢をとったか.
設問4. レトリック的大統領制とは何か. そして, レトリック的大統領制が登場するまで大統領と人民の関係はどのようなものであったか.

4. 革新主義の時代からニュー・ディールまで

Woodrow Wilson tried to perfect Roosevelt's methods of popular leadership and apply them in a way that would establish him as the leader of Congress and the Democratic Party. Wilson was not completely successful in this endeavor, but his two terms in office did bring about major changes in the presidency.

Appearances before Congress served Wilson's desire to break down the walls that long had divided the executive from the legislature. Although part of his purpose was to guide public opinion, he found it equally important to establish custom and make symbolic gestures that would strengthen the president's ties to Congress. Wilson's precedent-shattering speech was well received by most members of Congress.

World War I placed new demands on the war powers of the president. Waging a modern total war successfully required the mass production of complex weapons. The president became responsible for organizing and controlling the industrial economy and for coordinating the transportation and communication industries so they could meet the requirements of the military commitment. All this was in addition to the president's traditional duties as commander in chief of the armed forces.

After the peace negotiations, Wilson began the battle to ratify the Treaty of Versailles with little doubt that he would prevail. The conflict between Wilson and the Senate over the League of Nation may have been inevitable, rooted deeply in the country's traditional fear of entangling alliances. Wilson left on a month-long speaking tour. He hoped to create a popular groundswell that would force the Senate to ratify the treaty. The campaign was abortive because he suffered a severe stroke toward the end of the grueling trip.

Throughout most of the 1920s, reflecting widespread dissatisfaction with the expansion of federal functions during the Progressive Era and World War I, Warren G. Harding and Calvin Coolidge worked to curtail federal programs. Their policies contributed to nearly a decade of rapid economic growth, but weakened the regulatory state and undermined the strong, activist executive branch their predecessors had built.

The Great Depression struck with full force when the stock market crashed in October 1929, less than seven month after Herbert C. Hoover was inaugurated. Hoover put traditional, nineteenth-century American political creed, laissez-faire to the greatest test. But his unalterable commitment to preserving the tradition even in the face of national calamity severed only to discredit them.

Franklin D. Roosevelt had a clear and ambitious concept of what the role and function of the president should be. He believed that the complexities of a modern industrial, urban society required a stronger and more dynamic chief executive than the country had hitherto needed.

With the cooperation of a vigorous and well-led Congress, Roosevelt's eclectic program, dubbed the New Deal, employed federal funding and federal authority to a degree and with a scope seen hitherto only in war time. During Roosevelt's first one hundred days, the president invoked executive authority to declare a bank holiday, an action that probably saved the banking system from complete collapse. Congress passed a spate of laws, some in accordance with hastily drafted administration proposals. Measures to provide direct federal payments to the destitute, to restructure the country's system of agricultural production and marketing, and to encourage business-government cooperation in the industrial sector were passed. Innovative programs that reflected Roosevelt's particular interest in developing electrical power generation and in promoting conservation of natural resources were also adopted. Roosevelt declared the ideal of the New Deal in the first inaugural address as follows.

First Inaugural Address, March 4, 1933.
This great Nation will endure as it has endured, will revive and will prosper. So, first of all, let me assert my firm belief that the only thing we have to fear is fear itself—nameless, unreasoning, unjustified terror which paralyzes needed efforts to convert retreat into advance.

In every dark hour of our national life a leadership of frankness and vigor has met with that understanding and support of the people themselves which is essential to victory. I am convinced that you will again give that support to leadership in these critical days.

Roosevelt was a master of radio; his trademark broadcasts, dubbed Fireside Chats, appeared to establish a special bond between him and the American people. In march 1933, he first took to the airwaves to detail the government's step to shore up the banking system and thereafter used this medium to explain other complex problems in homey and accessible language.

Buoyed by his massive victory in the 1936 presidential election, Roosevelt devoted much of his second term to expanding and consolidating executive authority. Roosevelt sought to revamp the Supreme Court; to realign the political parties; and to strengthen executive authority.

In these efforts, he was at best only partly successful. His plan to expand membership on the Supreme Court failed. His efforts in the 1938 Democratic primary elections to replace conservative incumbent with New Dealers failed. But his ambitious plans to reorganize the executive branch partly succeeded. The Executive Office of the President was founded based on the proposal of the Brownlow Committee. It was designed as a presidential institution, responsible for tasks closely linked to the president's priorities and staffed by individuals who shared the president's political and policy objectives.

　The outbreak of war in Europe on September 1, 1939, and Japanese expansion into Southeast Asia drew attention away from domestic concerns. At the same time, Roosevelt's efforts to build up the American military and, later, to find ways to assist Great Britain as that country faced the threat of German invasion generated new opportunities to exercise presidential leadership and to concentrate power in the Oval Office. Throughout U.S. participation in the war, Roosevelt created myriad new agencies and programs to mobilize the country's resources. In December 1941, Congress granted the president vast wartime powers over the economy; throughout the war, Roosevelt employed them with resolve and vigor. Without legislative authorization, the chief executive launched such disparate initiatives as the Manhattan Project; the incarceration of more than one hundred thousand individuals of Japanese descent.

設問1. ウィルソンはどのようにして議会との画期的な関係を築いたのか.
設問2. ローズヴェルトはニュー・ディールで具体的にどのような対策を行ったのか.
設問3. ローズヴェルトは1936年の大統領選挙で勝利した後, どのように大統領の権限を拡大しようとしたのか.
設問4. ローズヴェルトは戦争権限で例えばどのようなことを行ったのか.

5. 冷戦と現代

Although his ascent to the presidency was unexpected, Harry S Truman significantly shaped American politics. Truman approved the National Security Act of 1947, which established the National Security Council, the Central Intelligence Agency, the Joint Chiefs of Staff, and the Department of Defense. The United States' containment strategy in the Cold War was developed in the Truman Administration, and it set the direction of American national security policy for the next four decades. In domestic policy, Truman expanded Roosevelt's New Deal programs with his own Fair Deal agenda, but he was less successful in enacting these policies. The Korean War started in 1950 and by the time he left office, in 1953, his approving ratings had dropped sharply.

Dwight D. Eisenhower largely adhered to the Truman administration's containment strategy, but with some important differences. To implement his policies, Eisenhower developed an extensive national security apparatus, with a Planning Board to prepare materials for weekly National Security Council meetings, and an Operations Coordinating Board to follow through on decisions. Eisenhower's organizational changes in the White House built upon his military experience and substantively influenced his policy choices, as is perhaps best illustrated by his systematic adoption of nuclear deterrence in the New Look.

John F. Kennedy was the first president to use television regularly as a venue for commutation, holding live, televised press conferences that boosted his public popularity. Television may well have contributed to Kennedy's 1960 victory over Richard M. Nixon, as the two candidates agreed to the first general-election presidential debates, and Kennedy was widely viewed as more comfortable and confident in that setting. Kennedy's steady leadership and carefully structured decision making during the Cuban Missile Crisis in 1962 defused what is considered the most significant confrontation between the two superpowers during the Cold War. In domestic policy, he used federal troops to enforce racial desegregation at the University of Mississippi and the University of Alabama.

The shocking circumstances that thrust Vice President Lyndon B. Johnson into the presidency overshadowed his administration and shaped his political legacy. He was committed to enacting Kennedy's policy agenda. He skillfully overcame opposition to the landmark Civil Rights Act of 1964. He had an ambitious domestic policy agenda which he called the Great Society, and which was intended to complete and expand upon the New Deal programs. He oversaw the creation of Medicare and Medicaid, federal programs that provide health care for the elderly and the poor, respectively. Despite Johnson's efforts to focus on domestic policy, his presidency would be remembered foremost for its involvement in the Vietnam War. The incremental escalation of American. troops in Vietnam took place without a congressional declaration of war, though in 1964, at Johnson's urging, Congress had passed the Gulf of Tonkin Resolution, which permitted the president to use military force to protect American interests in Southeast Asia.

The Nixon administration did successfully negotiate an end to the Vietnam War in 1973, but its military actions in the conflict continue to be highly controversial. Nixon visited China and the Soviet Union in 1972, and he signed two major arms control treaties with the Soviet Union. A Senate inquiry into the Watergate burglary in 1973 revealed the existence of the White House tapes, and this news provoked a major battle between Congress and the president over access to those conversations. Nixon insisted his executive privilege, and the case went to the Supreme Court, which ruled against the president. Facing almost certain impeachment in the House, Nixon resigned his office on August 9, 1974. The undeclared war on Vietnam and the Watergate scandal prompted charges of an "imperial presidency," and Congress subsequently tried to impose checks on what it viewed as abuses of presidential power. It passed the War

Powers Act of 1973, over Nixon's veto, and this legislation aimed to restrict the president's ability to send troops abroad without congressional approval.

Gerald R. Ford was a unique president. Never before had a vice president succeeded to the presidency because his predecessor resigned. Not only did Ford lack an electoral mandate, but he became president when the country was still deeply scarred by the Vietnam War, when respect for the presidency was greatly diminished.

Jimmy Carter is often described as an ineffective and miserable president, who alienated many Washington insiders and members of Congress. During his term, inflation and interest rates were at record highs, and the president was seen as ineffectual in domestic affairs and weak in foreign affairs. But, on the other hand, it can be said that Carter gave the country an administration that was marked by integrity and high-mindedness, despite severe constraints.

It seemed during the final days of the Carter administration that the presidency no longer worked. Of the five presidents who held office from 1961 to 1980, none completed two terms. In contrast to Ford and Carter, Ronald W. Reagan successfully advanced an ambitious legislative program in 1981 and 1982. From the beginning of his first term until the damaging revelations of the Iran-Contra affair in 1986, Reagan convinced most Americans that a strong, effective, popular leader had restored the presidency to preeminence in the political system. The oldest person to serve as president, he implemented a new style of leadership that downplayed his role as administrator and emphasized the use of news media to communicate with the public.

After the Iran-Contra scandal of the Reagan era, George H. W. Bush worked to restore integrity to the presidency. His presidency witnessed one of the most profound changes in international relations in the twentieth century. The Cold War ended with the collapse of the Soviet Union. The United States led an international coalition to victory in the Persian Gulf War against Iraq. In domestic affairs, however, he and Congress failed to arrive at a consensus on many issues. Bush inherited a large burden of debt and had to face the Democratic controlled Congress throughout his four years.

Bill Clinton devoted enormous energy in his first term to reforming the nation's health care system. He appointed First Lady Hillary Clinton to head the reform efforts. Her commission's proposed overhaul went down in resounding defeat. To make matters worse, a 1993 peacekeeping expedition to Somalia ended in fiasco. What's more, accusations had surfaced that the Clintons illegally profited from a phony land deal known as Whitewater. By late 1994, Clinton's popularity had plummeted, and the Democrats had lost control over Congress for the first time since the Truman administration.

But Clinton had regained the momentum. In 1996, he became the first Democrat to be reelected since Franklin D. Roosevelt. But the apparent turnaround was not to last. Allegations soon surfaced that Clinton had an inappropriate relationship with a young White House intern. When he denied it, the House began impeachment hearings against him. Clinton was eventually acquitted, but the presidency had been seriously damaged.

When George W. Bush took office, he persuaded Congress to approve the greatest tax cut since the Reagan administration. In foreign affairs, Bush shifted policy away from the direction that Clinton had followed. Generally distrustful of international treaties that he viewed as counter to American. self- interest, Bush rejected a long-sought agreement on global warming known as the Kyoto Protocol.

The September 11, 2001, terrorist attacks on New York City and Washington, D. C. shifted the focus of the administration. He pledged the nation the war on terrorism as follows.

Address to the Nation on the Terrorist Attacks, September 11, 2001.

Today our Nation saw evil, the very worst of human nature. And we responded with the best of America, with the daring of our rescue workers, with the caring for strangers and neighbors who came to give blood and help in any way they could.

I've directed the full resources of our intelligence and law enforcement communities to find those responsible and to bring them to justice. We will make no distinction between the terrorists who committed these acts and those who harbor them.

The war on terrorism affirmed the preeminence of the modern presidency. The new responsibilities that the war thrust on the executive led Bush to pursue major institutional reforms of the executive branch. In June 2002, Bush called for the creation of a Department of Homeland Security.

America's most celebrated presidents justified their reform programs in constitutional terms, claiming to restore the proper understanding of first principles even as they attempted to transfuse the Declaration and Constitution with new meaning. But they did so as great party leaders, in the midst of major partisan realignments. Critical contests between the parties—leavened by extraordinary presidential leadership—have enabled each generation to claim its right to redefine the Constitution's principles and reorganize its institutions. The burden of the twenty-first century is to hold the modern presidency to account by recapturing the understanding of democracy that has made such momentous debate and choice central to the pursuit of America's political destiny.

設問 1. トルーマン政権期に国家安全保障法で新設された機関は何か.
設問 2. ニクソン政権期に制定された戦争権限法の目的と内容は何か.
設問 3. ジョンソンの偉大なる社会とはどのような政策か.
設問 4. ブッシュが同時多発テロの後に新設した機関は何か.

解　答
1. 大統領制の起源と建国初期
設問 1. 大統領は選挙人によって選ばれる．選挙人の選出方法は各州に委ねられている．大統領に選ばれるためには選挙人の過半数を獲得する必要がある．

設問 2. 大統領に閣僚を罷免する権限を与える．

設問 3. ワシントンは国内の党派の分裂を警告した．さらにヨーロッパの同盟関係に巻き込まれることなくアメリカは独自の立場をとるべきだという孤立主義を提唱した．

2. ジェファソン・デモクラシー期から南北戦争
設問 1. ジェファソンは憲法上の問題はあったものの，ルイジアナ購入と出港禁止法を通じて大統領の権限を拡大した．

設問 2. 大統領選挙でサウス・カロライナを除いてすべての州で選挙人が一般投票で選出されるようになり，大統領が人民の代表であるという考えが現れた．ジャクソンは，官吏を政党に忠実な者に置き換えるという猟官制度を導入した．

設問 3. リンカンは戦争権限として議会の休会中に民兵を召集し，人身保護令状を差し止め，南部の港を封鎖し，連邦に忠実な者に武器を送った．

設問 4. ゲティスバーグ演説の意義は，久しくその重要性が忘れられていた独立宣言に基づき，以前とは違った新しい自由が連邦にもたらされたことを国民に広く知らせたことにある．

3. 南北戦争から革新主義の時代
設問 1. ペンドルトン法は猟官制度を是正する試みであり，連邦職員の採用や昇進に成果競争試験を課し，政治的査定を禁止する法律である．

設問 2. 19 世紀後半，アメリカの人口は急速に増大し，全国的な規模を持つ大企業が生まれた．こうした状況の中で大企業が政府を腐敗させ，個人の経済的自由が損なわれるのではないかという恐れが広がった．そうした考えが革新主義の発端となった．

設問 3. ローズヴェルトは「大統領は人民の世話役」という理念を持ち，大統領制を公共の福祉を確保するために使おうとした．しかし，ローズヴェルトは大企業の単なる敵であったわけではなく，大企業の行き過ぎを政府の規制を通じて抑えようとした．

設問 4. レトリック的大統領制は，人民に対するレトリックを大統領がリーダーシップを発揮する手段として利用するという制度である．それ以前は，大統領が人民に直接訴えかけるのは品位を損なう行為だと見なされていた．

4. 革新主義の時代からニュー・ディールまで

設問 1. ウィルソンは議会に自ら赴いて演説を行った．そうした試みは建国初期以来，ほとんど行われていなかった．

設問 2. 銀行休業令を出して銀行業の倒壊を防止した．貧困者に連邦による直接支援を行った．農業製品と市場制度を再構築した．工業部門で官民連携を推進した．電力開発事業を行い，天然資源保護を行った．

設問 3. ローズヴェルトは 3 つの手段を試した．ニュー・ディールを支持する判事を増やすために最高裁の定員を増やす．予備選挙で保守派の現職議員をニュー・ディール支持者に置き換える．行政組織の再編，大統領府を創設する．

設問 4. ローズヴェルトは原子爆弾を開発するマンハッタン計画を推進し，日系アメリカ人を強制収容した．

5. 冷戦と現代

設問 1. 国家安全保障会議，中央情報局，統合参謀本部，そして国防省が新設された．いずれも国家安全保障に重要な役割を果たしている．

設問 2. 戦争権限法は大統領の戦争権限の制限を目的にしている．その目的に基づいて，大統領が海外派兵を行う際に議会に報告するように求め，議会の承認が得られない場合は 60 日以内，もしくは最大で 90 日以内に軍隊を撤退させなければならないと規定している．

設問 3. 偉大なる社会はフランクリン・ローズヴェルトが行ったニュー・ディールに倣い，高齢者に対する医療保障と貧困者に対する医療扶助を提供した．

設問 4. 国土安全保障省が新設された．

第6章

オバマ政権と現代アメリカ
―― オバマ演説に見る光と影 ――

はじめに

バラク・フセイン・オバマ・ジュニア（Barack Hussein Obama, Jr.）は，ケニア出身の黒人を父に，カンザス州出身の白人を母に生まれた．そして，2008年の大統領選挙で当選し，黒人として初めてホワイトハウスの主人となった．こうして誕生した第44代大統領のオバマは，次のような経歴の持ち主で，2012年の大統領選挙でも再選を果たした．

Born（生年月日）：August 4, 1961 Honolulu, Hawaii, US
Political Party（政党）：Democratic
Spouse（配偶者）：Michelle Robinson（1992-現在）
Alma Mater（出身校）：Occidental College, Columbia University (B.A.), Harvard Law School (J.D.)
Profession（職業）：Community Organizer, Lawyer, Constitutional Law Professor
Religion（宗教）：Christian（キリスト教）
Awards（受賞）：2009 Nobel Peace Prize（2009年ノーベル平和賞）
Assumed Office（就任）：January 20, 2009
Vice President（副大統領）：Joe Biden
US Senator（連邦上院議員）from Illinois：January 3, 2005 – November 16, 2008（1期）
Member of the Illinois Senate（イリノイ州上院議員）from the 13th District：January 8, 1997 – November 4, 2004（3期）

1. 21世紀のアメリカとオバマの登場

アメリカ社会は，1980年代のロナルド・W・レーガン（Ronald W. Reagan）の時代から保守化傾向が強まり，「小さな政府」（small government），「新保守主義」（neo-conservatism），「新自由主義」（neo-liberalism）などの社会理念が強く押し出されてきた．それは，主に共和党が主導する政治体制であり，1993から2期8年間にわたって民主党のビル・クリントン（Bill Clinton）に政権を明け渡したとはいえ，共和党がレーガン政権から連邦政治の主導権を握ってきた．

1989年12月のマルタ会談によって冷戦の終焉が確認され，1991年12月に冷戦構造のライバルのソ連が崩壊すると，アメリカは，ポスト冷戦とグローバリゼーションの時代状況のなかで，次第に「単独行動主義」（ユニラテラリズムunilateralism）の外交姿勢を強めた．その分岐点となったのが，2001年の「9.11同時多発テロ」であった．

共和党のジョージ・W・ブッシュ（George W. Bush）は，第43代大統領として「9.11同時多発テロ」に対抗する強い政治姿勢を示し，2001年10月にはアフガニスタンのタリバーン軍事施設を攻撃した．そしてブッシュは，2002年1月の一般教書演説で北朝鮮，イラン，イラクを「悪の枢軸」（axis of evil）と非難すると，同年9月には「アメリカ国家安全保障戦略」（National Security Strategy），いわゆるブッシュ・ドクトリンを発表し，国際協調よりも軍事力を優先する「先制行動ドクトリン」を打ち出した．

この「アメリカ国家安全保障戦略」は，国連などの国際機関を中心とした「多国間主義」（multilateralism）ではなく，唯一の超大国となったアメリカが主導する「単独行動主義」の軍事ドクトリンであった．このようなブッシュ政権の軍事戦略は「新保守主義」の政治家ネオコンの影響を強く受けており，ブッシュ大統領は，2003年3月19日にイラクへ軍事侵攻し，サッダーム・H・フセイン（Saddam H. Hussein）政権を打倒する行動に出た．

しかし，民主党がこのようなブッシュ政権の強硬姿勢に手をこまねいていたわけではない．まだイリノイ州議会の上院議員であったオバマは，ブッシュ・ドク

第6章　オバマ政権と現代アメリカ ── オバマ演説に見る光と影 ──　115

トリンが出された直後の 2002 年 10 月 2 日，シカゴで「悲惨な結果と計り知れない犠牲」(Dire Consequences, Immeasurable Sacrifices) と題する演説を行い，ブッシュ政権がタリバーン政権を打倒したのに続き，フセイン政権への軍事攻撃を開始することに強く反対する姿勢を示した．この演説のなかで，オバマは何度も「私はすべての戦争に反対するものではない」(I don't oppose all war) と述べつつ，「私が反対するのは愚かな戦争だ」(What I am opposed to is a dumb war) と強調し，国連や国際世論を無視したブッシュ政権の外交姿勢を強く批判した．

　しかし，オバマの名前が全米に知れ渡り，一躍脚光を浴びるようになったのは，2004 年 7 月 26 ～ 28 日にボストンで行われた民主党全国大会であった．オバマは，この大会で「大いなる希望」(The Audacity of Hope) と題する基調演説 (Keynote Address) を行った．全米に流されたオバマ演説は，何度もスタンディング・オベーションを取るほど熱気に満ちたものであり，満場の民主党員を魅了し，大統領候補に選出されたジョン・F・ケリー (John F. Kerry) の演説がかすむほどであった．そのため，オバマを大統領にすべきという雰囲気も生まれ，2008 年の大統領選挙へとつながったと言われる．

　2001 年の「9.11 同時多発テロ」が起きた当初は，ブッシュ大統領の支持率は約 90％（ギャラップ調査）にも達していたが，アフガン・イラク戦争の犠牲者が増え続けるとともに莫大な財政負担が重くのしかかり，次第にブッシュ政権に対する批判が高まっていった．その結果，共和党主導の内政・外交に対する批判が強まり，財政赤字の拡大とともに国内世論も分裂状態となった．オバマ演説は，このような分裂したアメリカ社会をひとつにし，未来に向けて希望の光を投げかけるものだった．その終わりの方に，次のようなパラグラフがある．

　Yet even as we speak, (1)there are those who are preparing to divide us, the spin masters and negative ad peddlers who embrace the politics of anything goes. Well, I say to them tonight, there's not a liberal America and a conservative America – there's (2)the United States of America. There's not a black America and white America and (3)Latino America and Asian America; there's (2)the United States of America.　… (4)We are one people, all of us pledging allegiance to the stars and stripes, all of us defending the United States of America.

　民主党は，2000年の大統領選挙が一般投票の得票数で共和党を上回り，しかも開票結果に疑惑がもたれるほどの接戦であっただけに，2004年の大統領選挙で何としても雪辱を果たしたいと願っていた．しかし，結果的に政権奪還はならず，一般投票の得票比率からすると，1916年のウッドロー・ウィルソン（Woodrow Wilson）の再選を下回る，史上最低の僅差で現職のブッシュが再選された．

　ところが，フセイン放逐後のイラク情勢が混迷するとともに，国内では格差社会が顕在化し，ブッシュに対する支持率は急速に低下していった．2006年中間選挙の頃にはブッシュ支持率は約31％にまで落ち込み，中間選挙で民主党が12年ぶりに上下両院において多数を握った．そのため民主党は，2008年の大統領選挙に大きな期待をかけた．

　さらに，2007年夏頃には住宅バブルがはじけ，信用度の低いサブプライム・ローン（Subprime Lending/Subprime Mortgage）の返済が危機的な状況に陥った．このサブプライム・ローン危機はアメリカ経済に暗い影を落とし，2008年9月のリーマン・ブラザーズ（Lehman Brothers）の破綻から始まる金融危機へとつながった．連邦準備制度理事会（Federal Reserve Board）の元議長アラン・グリーンスパン（Alan Greenspan）は，この金融危機を前にして連邦議会で証言し，「我々は1世紀に1度の信用津波の真只中にいる」（We are in the midst of once-in-a century credit tsunami）と警鐘を鳴らした．

　このような社会情勢のなかで，当時連邦上院議員であったオバマは，早くも2007年2月10日，イリノイ州の州都スプリングフィールドで2008年の大統領選挙への出馬演説に臨んだ．イリノイ州はエイブラハム・リンカン（Abraham Lincoln）の出身州であり，オバマはスプリングフィールドの旧議事堂前で，「私たちの過去，未来，そしてアメリカのためのヴィジョン」（Our Past, Future & Vision for America）と題する出馬演説を行った．かつてリンカンは，ここで分裂した議会に団結を呼びかけたのであった．

　オバマは，「この国を変革させよう」（Let us transform this nation）と訴え，「こ

の困難な作業を共に始めよう」(Let us begin this hard work together) と呼びかけた．そしてオバマは，9回も繰り返して「…の世代となろう」(Let us be the generation...) と訴え続け，「新自由主義」の市場原理のもとで中産階級が分裂して格差社会が拡大し，強硬なテロ対策や中東情勢の混乱が反米感情を高めている現実を受け止め，政府と国民が一体となって未来志向の社会変革を実現しようと呼びかけた．

設問1．下線部（1）は，どのようなことを指していますか．
設問2．下線部（2）のようなフレーズを続けるオバマの意図は何ですか．
設問3．下線部（3）は，どのような人々を指していますか．
設問4．下線部（4）は，どのような意図が込められていますか．

2. 2008年大統領選挙とオバマ政権の発足

(1) 指名受諾演説

　2008年の大統領選挙は，イラク情勢の混迷と「100年に一度の経済危機」(worst recession in 100 years) という，深刻な内政・外交の危機を前に戦われた．共和党にとっては，ブッシュ政権の支持率低下と深刻な経済問題・金融危機からして，これまでにない強い「逆風」に晒された大統領選挙であった．ところが，有利なはずの民主党も，同じ上院議員のオバマとヒラリー・R・クリントン (Hillary R. Clinton) が候補指名争いのデッドヒートを繰り返し，党内に泥仕合にも似た激しい意見対立が起きた．

　しかし，2008年6月3日の予備選挙最終日，モンタナとサウスダコタ両州の予備選挙でオバマが過半数の代議員を獲得し，同年8月25日からコロラド州デンバーで開かれた民主党全国大会は，ついに最終日の28日，初めて黒人のオバマを大統領候補に指名した．45年前 (1963年) のこの日，人種差別に反対する「ワシントン大行進」が行われ，マーチン・ルーサー・キング (Martin Luther King, Jr.) が，有名な「私には夢がある」(I have a dream) と演説した．

　オバマは，「アメリカの約束」(The American Promise) と題する指名受諾演

説のなかで，現在のアメリカが決定的な節目にあると訴え，経済的混乱のために生活が苦しく，夢や希望が失われつつあることを率直に認め，政府の役割が十分に発揮されていないと，ブッシュ政権を批判した．

We meet at one of those defining moments – a moment when our nation is at war, our economy is in turmoil, and the American promise has been threatened once more.

Tonight, (1)more Americans are out of work and more are working harder for less. More of you have lost your homes and even more are watching your home values plummet. (2)More of you have cars you can't afford to drive, credit card bills you can't afford to pay, and tuition that's beyond your reach.

These challenges are not all of government's making. (3)But the failure to respond is a direct result of a broken politics in Washington and the failed policies of George W. Bush.…

オバマは，「今回の大統領選挙がアメリカの約束を 21 世紀にも生かすため大きなチャンスだ」(This election is our chance to keep, in the 21st century, the American promise alive) と有権者に訴え，「11 月 4 日には私たちは立ち上がって，『(共和党の) 8 年でもうたくさんだ』といわなければならない」(On November 4th, we must stand up and say: "Eight is enough") と，民主党への支持を熱烈に呼びかけた．

政権与党の共和党は，2000 年の大統領選挙で旋風を巻き起こした上院議員のジョン・マケイン (John McCain) を大統領候補に立てた．オバマは，マケインがブッシュ政権下でアメリカ経済が大きく伸びた，経済のファンダメンタルズ (基礎的条件) がしっかりしている，などと主張する楽観論を強く批判した．

The truth is, on issue after issue that would make a difference in your lives – on health care and education and the economy – Senator McCain has been anything but independent. He said that (4)our economy has made "great progress" under this President. He said that (5)the fundamentals of the economy are strong. And when one of his chief advisors – the man who wrote his economic plan – was talking about the anxiety Americans are feeling, he said that we were just suffering from (6)a "mental recession," and that we've become, and I quote, "a nation of whiners."

オバマは，マケインが「20年以上も，すでに否定された古臭い共和党哲学にこだわってきた」(For over two decades, he's subscribed to that old, discredited Republican philosophy) と攻撃し，それが「…富めるものにもっともっと与えることで豊かさが少しでもほかのみんなに染みわたるよう期待する」(give more and more to those with the most and hope that prosperity trickles down to everyone else) 社会理念だと批判した．確かに，当時の共和党は，「新自由主義」の社会理念のもとで自立・自助の精神を高め，「持てる者の社会」(Ownership Society) を実現するという政策理念を掲げていた．

オバマは，「アメリカよ，今は小さな計画を立てるときではない」(America, now is not the time for small plans) と呼びかけ，雇用機会を増やす企業の法人税減免，勤労世帯の95％に対する減税，10年以内に中東への石油依存からの脱却などの政策を具体的に提示した．しかもオバマは，環境・エネルギー政策と地球温暖化・気候変動対策にも力をいれ，当選後に打ち出されることになる「グリーン・ニューディール」(Green New Deal) のアイデアが早くも示された．

As President, I will tap our natural gas reserves, invest in clean coal technology, and find ways to safely harness nuclear power. I'll help our auto companies re-tool, so that (7)the fuel-efficient cars of the future are built right here in America. I'll make it easier for the American people to afford these new cars. And I'll invest 150 billion dollars over the next decade in affordable, (8)renewable sources of energy – wind power and solar power and the next generation of biofuels; an investment that will lead to new industries and five million new jobs that pay well and can't ever be outsourced.

さらにオバマは，「今こそ国民への約束を守り，すべての国民に安く使いやすい医療保険をついに提供するときだ」(Now is the time to finally keep the promise of affordable, accessible health care for every single American) と述べ，「将来世代のために社会保障制度を守るべき時」(the time to protect Social Security for future generations) だと強調した．しかし，そのためには財政基盤

の確立が必要であり，すでに 2008 会計年度（07 年 10 月～ 08 年 9 月）に 4,550 億ドル（前年度比 2,930 億ドル増）にまで膨れ上がった財政赤字の削減が不可欠であるとし，オバマは，「連邦政府予算を一行ずつしらみつぶしにして，無駄で無用な政府事業を排除する」(But I will also go through the federal budget, line by line, eliminating programs that no longer work) と，財政再建への強い姿勢を示した．

そしてオバマは，「私は立ち上がってこの戦争に反対した」(I stood up and opposed this war) と述べ，ブッシュ政権が開始したイラク戦争を批判し，イラク情勢の混迷を終結させる強い姿勢を示した．

(9)As Commander-in-Chief, I will never hesitate to defend this nation, but I will only send our troops into harm's way with a clear mission and a sacred commitment to give them the equipment they need in battle and the care and benefits they deserve when they come home.

(10)I will end this war in Iraq responsibly, and finish the fight against Al Qaeda and the Taliban in Afghanistan. …But I will also renew the tough, direct diplomacy that can prevent Iran from obtaining nuclear weapons and curb Russian aggression. (11)I will build new partnerships to defeat the threats of the 21st century: terrorism and nuclear proliferation; poverty and genocide; climate change and disease.

また，オバマは社会問題も取り上げ，妊娠中絶（abortion）の容認，銃規制の強化，ゲイ・レズビアン（gay and lesbian）の権利承認，不法移民への柔軟な対応などの方針を示した．そして，最後にオバマは，「私たちは後ろを振り向くわけには行かない」(we cannot turn back) と繰り返し，1963 年の「ワシントン大行進」のように，人種や信条を超えて未来への「約束」を実現させようと呼びかけた．

(2) 勝利演説

イラク情勢の泥沼化やサブプライム・ローン危機によって，ブッシュの支持率は 2008 年 2 月には 19% にまで低下しており，不支持率も 70% 台後半になって

いたため,共和党にとって 2008 年の大統領選挙は強い「逆風」を受けていた. しかも,一般投票を 2 カ月後に控えた 9 月 15 日には,全米証券業界第 4 位の名門投資銀行リーマン・ブラザーズ (Lehman Brothers) が約 6,130 億ドルの負債を抱えて破綻し,全米に深刻な金融危機がひろがる事態となった.

その結果,11 月 4 日の一般投票では,「変革」(change) と「そうだ,私たちにはできる」(Yes, we can) というスローガンを掲げる民主党のオバマ陣営 (副大統領はジョー・バイデン) が,「国が第一」(country first) をスローガンとする共和党のマケイン陣営 (副大統領候補はサラ・ペイリン Sarah Palin) を大差で破った. オバマは,当選が決まった 4 日の夜,地元シカゴのグラント・パークで約 20 万人の支持者を前に,「アメリカに変化がやってきた」(Change has come to America) と呼びかける勝利演説を行った.

オバマは,「今夜のこの勝利が真に誰のものなのか,私は決して忘れない. この勝利は,みなさんのものだ」(I will never forget who this victory truly belongs to‐it belongs to you) と,初めて黒人が大統領に当選したことを称えた. そしてオバマは,次のように必ずしも有力候補でなかった自らを振り返り,ヒラリー・クリントンとの指名争いや民主党内の亀裂を乗り越え,若い世代の「草の根」(grass-root) 運動と選挙資金集めによって勝利を果たしたと強調し,「これは皆さんの勝利だ」(This is your victory) と訴えた.

(12)I was never the likeliest candidate for this office. We didn't start with much money or many endorsements. Our campaign was not hatched in the halls of Washington….

It was built by working men and women who dug into what little savings they had to give five dollars and ten dollars and twenty dollars to this cause. It grew strength from the young people who rejected the myth of their generation's apathy; who left their homes and their families for jobs that offered little pay and less sleep; from the not-so-young people who braved the bitter cold and scorching heat to (13)knock on the doors of perfect strangers; from (14)the millions of Americans who volunteered, and organized, and proved that more than two centuries later, (15)a government of the people, by the people and for the people has not perished from this Earth. This is your victory.

　オバマは,「私たちは, 明日からこの時代最大の課題に取り組まなくてはならない」(we know the challenges that tomorrow will bring are the greatest of our lifetime) と訴え, アフガン・イラクの2つの戦争と「100年に一度の経済危機」という大きな課題に取り組む姿勢を強調した. オバマは, アフガン・イラク情勢について,「…イラクの砂漠とアフガニスタンの山岳でいま目覚めようとする勇敢なアメリカ人たちがおり, 彼らが私たちのために命を危険にさらしている」(…there are brave Americans waking up in the deserts of Iraq and the mountains of Afghanistan to risk their lives for us) と指摘した.

　金融危機については,「今回の金融危機から得た教訓というのは, メーン・ストリート (普通の町の中央通り) が苦しんでいるのにウォール・ストリートだけ栄えるなど, そんなことがあってはならないということを忘れずにいよう」(Let us remember that if this financial crisis taught us anything, it's that we cannot have a thriving Wall Street while Main Street suffers) と強調した.

　オバマは,「この国の私たちは, ひとつの国として, ひとつの国民として, 共に栄え, 共に苦しむ」(in this country, we rise or fall as one nation, as one people) はずなのに, 共和党政権が格差と分断の社会を生み出してしまったと批判し,「…今夜, 民主党は確かに大きな勝利を獲得したが, 私たちはいささか謙虚に, そして決意をもって, この国の前進を阻んでいた分断を癒すつもりだ」(…while the Democratic Party has won a great victory tonight, we do so with a measure of humility and determination to heal the divides that have held back our progress) と述べた.

　そしてオバマは, このような課題を解決する道のりが険しいことを承知しつつ,「みなさんに約束する. 私たちは, ひとつの国民として, 必ずたどり着く」(I promise you - we as a people will get there) と, 早くも2期目に向けた強い意欲を示した. しかも,「アメリカのリーダーシップはもうすぐ, 新たな夜明けを迎える」(a new dawn of American leadership is at hand) と強調し,「この世界を破壊しようとする者たちに告げる. われわれはお前たちを打ち破る」(To those who would tear this world down - we will defeat you) と, 安全保障とテ

第6章 オバマ政権と現代アメリカ —— オバマ演説に見る光と影 —— 123

ロ対策に強い姿勢を示した．そして，最後にオバマは，何度も「そうだ，私たちにはできる」(Yes, we can) を繰り返し，自らの勝利演説を締めくくった．

(3) 就任演説

オバマは，2009年1月20日，第44代大統領の就任式に臨んだ．第44回就任式のテーマは，リンカンの生誕200年を記念して，「自由の新しい誕生」(A New Birth of Freedom) とされた．この日は，気温が零下7度と厳しい寒さのなか，議事堂からリンカン記念堂付近には200万人を超える人々が集まった．

オバマは，連邦憲法の冒頭にある「私たち人民」(We the people) を引用しつつ，経済危機に直面する国民に努力と勤勉を求め，アメリカ建国の理想と信念を掲げ続けようと呼びかけた．そしてオバマは，「私たちが危機の最中にあることは今や周知のことだ」(That we are in the midst of crisis is now well understood) と述べ，アフガン・イラク両戦争のツケ，金融資本主義の強欲さなどがアメリカ経済を弱体化させたと批判した．現在のアメリカでは，経済が弱体化したために会社が破綻し，国民は家や仕事を失い，教育が行き詰まり，高すぎる医療保険に加入できない国民が多いと訴えた．

…(16)Our nation is at war, against a far-reaching network of violence and hatred. (17)Our economy is badly weakened, a consequence of greed and irresponsibility on the part of some, but also our collective failure to make hard choices and prepare the nation for a new age. Homes have been lost; jobs shed; businesses shuttered. Our health care is too costly; our schools fail too many; and each day brings further evidence that the ways we use energy strengthen our adversaries and threaten our planet.

しかしオバマは，自信を喪失したり，恐怖心を抱いたりすることなく，「今こそ，私たちの不屈の精神を再確認する時だ」(The time has come to reaffirm our enduring spirit) と呼びかけ，「今日から私たちは，自力で立ち上がり，…アメリカを再生するため再び働き始めなくてはならない」(Starting today, we must pick ourselves up,…and begin again the work of remaking America)と強調した．

オバマは，新たな雇用創出，社会インフラの整備，科学技術の振興，再生可能

エネルギーの活用，教育改革の実現などの課題に取り組む姿勢を示した．しかも，そのためには，政府が十分な機能や役割を発揮し，国民との間に信頼関係を築かなければならないと述べた．

(18)The question we ask today is not whether our government is too big or too small, but whether it works - whether it helps families find jobs at a decent wage, care they can afford, a retirement that is dignified. …And those of us who manage the public's dollars will be held to account - to spend wisely, reform bad habits, and do our business in the light of day – (19)because only then can we restore the vital trust between a people and their government.

オバマは，金融危機と不況の蔓延が「新自由主義」（ネオ・リベラリズム）による市場競争の暴走にあるとみなし，野放図な自由競争や市場原理に対して警鐘を鳴らした．

Nor is the question before us whether the market is a force for good or ill. Its power to generate wealth and expand freedom is unmatched, but (20)this crisis has reminded us that without a watchful eye, the market can spin out of control - and that a nation cannot prosper long when it favors only the prosperous. (21)The success of our economy has always depended not just on the size of our Gross Domestic Product, but on the reach of our prosperity; on our ability to extend opportunity to every willing heart - not out of charity, but because it is the surest route to our common good.

安全保障の問題では，「私たちは再び世界をリードする用意ができている」（we are ready to lead once more）と強調し，イラク・アフガニスタンに平和と安定をもたらすとともに，核の脅威とテロ撲滅に次のような強い姿勢を表明した．

We will begin to responsibly leave Iraq to its people, and forge a hard-earned peace in Afghanistan. With old friends and former foes, we will work tirelessly to (22)lessen the nuclear threat, and roll back the specter of a warming planet. …and for those who seek to advance their aims by (23)inducing terror and slaughtering innocents, we say to you now that our spirit is stronger and cannot be broken; you cannot outlast us, and we will defeat you.

第6章　オバマ政権と現代アメリカ ── オバマ演説に見る光と影 ──　*125*

　オバマは，アメリカが多宗教・多文化・多人種を享受してきた国であり，貧困撲滅や環境・エネルギー対策などのグローバルな課題を世界と共有していく姿勢を示した．しかし，そのために「私たちに今求められているのは，新しい責任の時代」(What is required of us now is a new era of responsibility) であり，「すべてのアメリカ人が，自分自身，国家，そして世界に対して義務を負っていると認識」(a recognition, on the part of every American, that we have duties to ourselves, our nation, and the world) することが重要だと訴え，「これこそが市民としての負担と約束だ」(This is the price and the promise of citizenship) と強調した．

設問 1．下線部（1）は，どのようなことを指していますか．
設問 2．下線部（2）は，生活面で，どのようなことを指していますか．
設問 3．下線部（3）は，政治面で，どのようなことを指していますか．
設問 4．下線部（4）は，どのようなことを指していますか．
設問 5．下線部（5）は，経済面で，どのようなことを指していますか．
設問 6．下線部（6）は，具体的に，どのようなことを指していますか．
設問 7．下線部（7）は，どのようなことを指していますか．
設問 8．下線部（8）は，具体的に，どのようなエネルギーを指していますか．
設問 9．下線部（9）は何を意味し，実際に誰を指していますか．
設問 10．下線部（10）は，どのようなことを指していますか．
設問 11．下線部（11）は，具体的に，どのようなことを指していますか．
設問 12．下線部（12）は，どのようなことを指していますか．
設問 13．下線部（13）は，具体的に，どのようなことを指していますか．
設問 14．下線部（14）は，具体的に，どのようなことを指していますか．
設問 15．下線部（15）のフレーズから，どのようなことを連想しますか．
設問 16．下線部（16）は，どのようなことを指していますか．
設問 17．下線部（17）は，経済面で，どのようなことを指していますか．
設問 18．下線部（18）は，どのようなことを指していますか．
設問 19．下線部（19）は，どのようなことを指していますか．

設問 20. 下線部（20）は，具体的に，どのようなことを指していますか.
設問 21. 下線部（21）は，経済面で，どのようなことを指していますか.
設問 22. 下線部（22）は，どのようなことを指していますか.
設問 23. 下線部（23）は，どのようなことを指していますか.

3. 第1期オバマ政権の実績

　ブッシュ政権のもとで，2008年10月3日に緊急経済安定化法（Emergency Economic Stabilization Act）が成立し，最大約7,000億ドルの公的資金を投入して金融機関の不良債権を買い取ることになった．ところが，深刻な金融危機が実体経済に大きなダメージを与えることが不可避となり，オバマ新大統領は，就任直後の2009年2月13日，総額7,872億ドル規模の景気対策を柱とするアメリカ再生・再投資法（American Recovery and Reinvestment Act）を成立させた．
　しかし，世界同時不況と言われるほど景気後退が深刻な事態となったため，アメリカの失業率は約9％前後で高止まりし，雇用拡大と景気回復に明るい兆しが見えなかった．しかも，一向にアフガン・イラク情勢は安定せず，2009年度の財政赤字も1兆4,130億ドル（対GDP比約10％）に達した．その結果，就任当初から約70％前後を維持してきたオバマ大統領の支持率は，2009年6月のギャラップ調査では58％にまで下落した．

(1)「核のない世界」演説
　オバマは，ブッシュ政権下で亀裂を生じた欧州諸国との同盟関係を再構築するため，2009年4月に開かれた，ロンドンの20カ国・地域（G20）首脳会議（第2回金融サミット）とフランス・ストラスブールの北大西洋条約機構（NATO）首脳会議に出席した．そしてオバマは，欧州訪問の最後に冷戦や東西関係の結節点となったチェコを訪問し，4月5日に有名な「核のない世界」（A World without Nuclear Weapons）を行った．演説は，チェコスロバキアの初代大統領マサリクの銅像がある，首都プラハのフラッチャニ広場で行われた．
　オバマは，「21世紀の核兵器の未来」（the future of nuclear weapons in the

21st century）について，次のように熱っぽく語った．

Today, the Cold War has disappeared but thousands of those weapons have not. In a strange turn of history, (1)the threat of global nuclear war has gone down, but the risk of a nuclear attack has gone up. More nations have acquired these weapons. Testing has continued. (2)Black market trade in nuclear secrets and nuclear materials abound. The technology to build a bomb has spread. Terrorists are determined to buy, build or steal one. Our efforts to contain these dangers are centered on a global non-proliferation regime, but as more people and nations break the rules, (3)we could reach the point where the center cannot hold.

オバマは，核をめぐる厳しい現実に対処するために強力な指導力を発揮すると訴え，アメリカが核兵器のない世界を追求すると約束した．

And as nuclear power—as a nuclear power, (4)as the only nuclear power to have used a nuclear weapon, the United States has a moral responsibility to act. We cannot succeed in this endeavor alone, but we can lead it, we can start it.

So today, I state clearly and with conviction (5)America's commitment to seek the peace and security of a world without nuclear weapons. I'm not naive. This goal will not be reached quickly—perhaps not in my lifetime. It will take patience and persistence. But now we, too, must ignore the voices who tell us that the world cannot change. We have to insist, "Yes, we can."

オバマは，安全保障戦略における核兵器の比重を下げるため，①ロシアと新たな戦略兵器削減条約の交渉開始，②包括的核実験禁止条約（Comprehensive Nuclear Test Ban Treaty：CTBT）の早期批准，③「核兵器用核分裂物質生産禁止（カットオフ）条約」（Fissile Material Cut-off Treaty）の交渉開始などの方針が示された．さらに，核不拡散防止条約（Nuclear Non-Proliferation Treaty：NPT）体制を強化するため，①民生用の核燃料を国際管理する国際核燃料バンク（International Fuel Bank）構想推進，②世界中の無防備な核物質を4年以内に安全なものとする国際的枠組みの構築，③大量破壊兵器拡散防止構想（Proliferation Security Initiative：PSI）と対テロ構想の国際機関化などの具体

案を提唱した．

そして，2009年9月には国連安全保障理事会（United Nations Security Council）で核不拡散・核軍縮に関する首脳会談が開かれ，オバマ大統領の提案によって「核のない世界」をめざす決議が全会一致で採択された．この安保理決議は，オバマがプラハの「核のない世界」演説で示した構想に世界が同意したことの表れであった．安保理では同様の首脳会談が1992年以降それまでに計5回開かれていたが，核不拡散・核軍縮に特化した議論はまだ前例がなく，アメリカの大統領が議長を務めリードした会談も初めてのことであった．

(2) ノーベル平和賞受賞演説

ノーベル賞委員会は，このようなオバマの「核のない世界」をめざす強い姿勢を評価し，2009年10月9日にオバマにノーベル平和賞を授与すると発表した．

しかし，オバマはまだ核廃絶への道筋に具体的な実績をあげておらず，本人も平和賞の候補に挙がっていることすら知らなかったと言われる．そのため，各方面から受賞決定に関して賛否両論が渦巻き，2009年12月10日にオスロで行われた「正しい戦争，正しい平和」（Just War, Just Peace）と題する受賞演説も，オバマの理想論と現実論が交錯するものとなった．当時オバマは，同年12月1日に3万人増派（駐留米軍約10万人）を中心とするアフガニスタン新戦略を発表したばかりだった．

オバマは，「現在もアメリカはまだ戦争をしている」（Still, we are at war）と述べ，「私の受賞に関する最大の問題は，私が（アフガン・イラクの）二つの戦争をおこなっている国家の軍最高司令官だということだ」（the most profound issue surrounding my receipt of this prize is the fact that I am the Commander-in-Chief of the military of a nation in the midst of two wars）と，率直に国際世論の批判に応えた．

オバマは，キングやマハトマ・ガンジー（Mahatma Gandhi）が非暴力の姿勢を貫き，世界の平和に大きく貢献したことを賞賛しつつも，非暴力ではアドルフ・ヒトラー（Adolf Hitler）の軍隊を止められなかったし，単なる交渉ではアル・カーイダの武器を放棄させられないと主張した．そのためオバマは，「私は

人道的理由による武力行使は正当化できると信じている」(I believe that force can be justified on humanitarian grounds) と述べた.

　オバマは,「単独であろうと他国と共同であろうと, 武力の行使が必要なばかりでなく道義的にも正当化されると国家が考える場合がある」(There will be times when nations—acting individually or in concert—will find the use of force not only necessary but morally justified) と述べ,「戦争という手段は平和を維持するうえでひとつの役割を果たすものだ」(the instruments of war do have a role to play in preserving the peace) と認めた.

　しかしオバマは,「戦争自体は決して輝かしいものではなく」(war itself is never glorious),「戦争は人間に悲劇をもたらす」(war promises human tragedy) と述べ,「正しい戦争とは何か, 正しい平和を実現するには何が必要なのかということについて, 新しい考え方が求められている」(it will require us to think in new ways about the notions of just war and the imperatives of a just peace) と訴えた.

　そして, オバマは, 世界の安全保障に対するアメリカの姿勢を強調し, 次のように国連やNATOの役割を強化することを求めた.

　　America's commitment to global security will never waver. But in a world in which threats are more diffuse, and missions more complex, (6)America cannot act alone. America alone cannot secure the peace. This is true in Afghanistan. This is true in failed states like Somalia, where terrorism and piracy is joined by famine and human suffering. …

　　The leaders and soldiers of NATO countries, and other friends and allies, demonstrate this truth through the capacity and courage they've shown in Afghanistan. …(7)Peace requires responsibility. Peace entails sacrifice. That's why NATO continues to be indispensable. That's why we must strengthen U.N. and regional peacekeeping, and not leave the task to a few countries.

　最後にオバマは, 正しく永続的な平和を構築する3つの方法を提示した. それは, 第一に武力行使以外の制裁措置と核拡散の防止を強化すること, 第二に人間の固有の権利と尊厳に基づく「正しい平和」(just peace) を求め続けること,

第三に市民的・政治的権利だけでなく経済的な安定や機会を保障すること，だった．

(3) 医療保険制度改革演説

オバマの支持率が下落した重要な要因のひとつに，共和党を始めとする保守派が医療保険制度の改革に強く反対したことがあった．2009年8月に民主党が全国各地で開いたタウン・ミーティングでは，「ティーパーティ運動」(Tea Party Movement) などに現れた「草の根」保守派が，医療保険制度に公的保険の選択肢（パブリック・オプション）を導入するプランを「社会主義」の制度化であると攻撃した．その結果，タウン・ミーティングは怒号の飛び交う集会となり，医療保険改革は政策の選択ではなく，保守対リベラルの政治的なイデオロギー対決になった．

オバマは，2009年9月9日，上下両院合同会議で異例の演説を行い，過剰なイデオロギー対立を乗り越え，民主・共和両党の妥協を促す手段に出た．オバマは，無保険者が約4,900万人（国民の16％超）にのぼり，3人に1人が保険の加入を拒否されている現状を訴え，「多くの人々をそんな状態に放置している先進民主主義国，豊かな国は，この世界でアメリカ以外にどこにもない」(We are the only advanced democracy on Earth – the only wealthy nation – that allows such hardships for millions of its people) と呼びかけた．これは，民主・共和両党が固定観念やイデオロギー対立を排して，「今や医療保険改革を成し遂げる時」(Now is the time to deliver on healthcare) という，オバマの強い姿勢を受け止めてほしいと訴えるものだった．

オバマは，医療保険改革の目標として既保険の安定化，無保険者の解消，医療費の抑制の3つを上げ，「個人は基本的な医療保険に加入することが義務化され」(individuals will be required to carry basic health insurance)，「すべての人が自分の分を果たす」(everybody does their part) ことによって医療保険改革が実現すると強調した．

オバマの医療保険改革（オバマケア）では，特に無保険の個人や零細企業が公的な保障を受ける保険を選択できる，いわゆるパブリック・オプションが，医療

保険全体を「政府が乗っ取る」(government takeover) ものであるという批判が強まった．これに対してオバマは，パブリック・オプションが無保険者のための選択肢であり，強制的なものではないと強調し，パブリック・オプションに加入するのは国民の5%未満にすぎないと断言した．

　アメリカには，政府が管掌するメディケイド（低所得者・身体障害者医療扶助）とメディケア（高齢者医療保険）がある．オバマケアはこれを守るとともに，非効率な部分と無駄をなくし，上昇し続けている医療コストを引き下げ，将来的には財政負担を減らすことができると強調した．

　Add it all up, and (8)the plan I'm proposing will cost around $900 billion over ten years – less than we have spent on the Iraq and Afghanistan wars, and less than the tax cuts for the wealthiest few Americans that Congress passed at the beginning of the previous administration. (9)Most of these costs will be paid for with money already being spent – but spent badly – in the existing health-care system. The plan will not add to our deficit. The middle-class will realize greater security, not higher taxes. And if we are able to slow the growth of health care costs by just one-tenth of 1.0% each year, (10)it will actually reduce the deficit by $4 trillion over the long term.

　オバマケアは，大統領自身の強いリーダーシップのもと，連邦議会で多数を握る民主党が結束し，2009年末までに上下両院で関連法案を通過させた．そして，2010年3月に両院協議会のすり合せが行われた結果，患者保護・医療費負担適正化法（Patient Protection and Affordable Act）と医療・教育負担抑制調整法（Health Care and Education Reconciliation Act）を柱とする医療保険改革が制度化された．

(4) オバマの苦悩

　就任から1年目を迎えた2010年1月，オバマは冷たい「逆風」を受けながら一般教書演説を行った．「大きな政府」「社会主義」などという保守派からの批判が絶えず，財政出動による景気回復も十分に進まないため，オバマ政権が発足してから400万人以上が職を失い，2009年10月には失業率が26年ぶりに2桁の

10.2％に突入した.

しかも，イラク・アフガンの戦費関連支出が重くのしかかり，2011 年会計年度の財政赤字は，過去最高の 1 兆 6,450 億ドル（対 GDP 比 10.9％）にも達した．その結果，オバマ大統領の支持率は 2011 年 9 月には過去最低の 43％にまで下落し，ニューヨークで「ウォール街を占拠せよ」（Occupy Wall Street）の抗議運動が始まり，全米各地で格差社会を批判するデモが広がりを見せた．

このようなオバマ政権に対する期待感の喪失は，すでに 2010 年 11 月の中間選挙にも如実に表れた．この中間選挙で民主党は，上院でかろうじて過半数を維持したものの，下院では共和党に 65 議席も躍進を許す歴史的敗北を喫し，共和党が 4 年ぶりに過半数の議席を制した．その結果，オバマ政権は「分割政治」（divided government）の局面に立たされ，議会対策に以前よりも困難さが増した．

設問 1．下線部（1）は，具体的に，どのようなことを指していますか．
設問 2．下線部（2）は，具体的に，どのようなことを指していますか．
設問 3．下線部（3）は，具体的に，どのようなことを指していますか．
設問 4．下線部（4）は，アメリカの責任をどのように述べていますか．
設問 5．下線部（5）は，アメリカの立場をどのように述べていますか．
設問 6．下線部（6）は，どのようなことを指していますか．
設問 7．下線部（7）は，どのようなことを指していますか．
設問 8．下線部（8）は，具体的に，どのようなことを指していますか．
設問 9．下線部（9）は，具体的に，どのようなことを指していますか．
設問 10．下線部（10）は，具体的に，どのようなことを指していますか．

4．オバマ再選への道

オバマは，早くも 2011 年 4 月に 2012 年の大統領選挙への出馬を表明し，「我々は長く続く変化が簡単にはやってこないことを知っている」（We've always known that lasting change wouldn't come quickly or easily）と述べ，引き続き

政策の継続を訴えた．このような姿勢は，すでに同年1月25日に行われた一般教書演説にも表れており，オバマは，「だが，為すべきことはまだある．…未来を勝ち取るためには，何十年にもわたって続いてきた試練に取り組む必要がある」(But we have to do more. …but to win the future, we'll need to take on challenges that have been decades in the making) と強調した．

しかし，失業率の改善や雇用拡大が思うように進まないため，2011年10月3日に行われたABCテレビとのインタビューで，オバマは4年前よりも社会状況が悪くて再選への道が険しいことを認め，「私は負け犬になることに慣れている」(I'm used to being the underdog) と漏らした．だが，民主党側にオバマに対抗する有力候補者が生まれず，2012年9月3日～6日にノースカロライナ州シャーロットで開かれた全国大会では，オバマが再び大統領候補に指名された．

指名受諾演説に立ったオバマは，多数の「中間層」(middle class) の生活を建て直し，2016年までに製造業の分野で100万人の雇用を創出すると約束した．また，今後10年のうちに財政赤字を4兆ドル削減すること，そして，2020年までに石油の輸入を半減させることなどの具体的な政策目標も示した．最後にオバマは，「私たちは後戻りしない．私たちは誰も取り残さない」(We don't turn back. We leave no one behind) と訴えた．

(1) 再選勝利演説

民主党は現職のオバマとバイデンが再選を賭けて大統領選挙を戦うことになったが，共和党は一足先に2012年8月27日～30日にフロリダ州タンパで全国大会を開き，前マサチューセッツ州知事のミット・ロムニー (Mitt Romney) と下院予算委員会委員長のポール・ライアン (Paul Ryan, Jr.) を正副大統領候補に選出した．民主党全国大会がオバマを候補者に正式決定した頃には，僅差でロムニー陣営有利という世論調査の結果もでていた．

ところが，11月6日に行われた大統領選挙の一般投票では，オバマ：50.5%（選挙人332），ロムニー：47.9%（同206）という，予想外の大差でオバマが再選された．これは，オバマが旋風を巻き起こした2008年の大統領選挙ほどではないものの，政策の継続を訴えたことが民主党にとっては大きな勝因であった．

なお，大統領選挙で民主党の候補者が1期目と2期目の一般投票でともに50％を超える得票をしたのは，大恐慌の真只中の1932・36年以来久々のことである．

再選を果たしたオバマ大統領は，11月7日の未明，シカゴのマコーミック・コンヴェンション・センターで，1万人の支援者を前に勝利演説を行った．オバマは，冒頭で「私たちの団結をより完成させるための仕事がさらに前進する」(the task of perfecting our union moves forward) と述べ，「皆さんのおかげで前進する」(It moves forward because of you) と，2期目の政権運営に強い意欲を見せた．しかし，大統領選挙の同時に行われた上下両院議員選挙では，上院は民主党，下院は共和党が多数を占める「分割政治」が続くことになり，オバマは，次のように共和党と協力する超党派の姿勢を示した．

And in the coming weeks and months, I am looking forward to reaching out and working with leaders of both parties to meet the challenges we can only solve together – (1)reducing our deficit, (2)reforming out tax code, (3)fixing our immigration system, (4)freeing ourselves from foreign oil. (5)We've got more work to do.

オバマ陣営は，製造業の再建によって100万人の雇用創出を実現すると公約し，「私たちはひとつの家族」(We are an American family) の立場から中間層を重視するとともに，財政再建のために富裕層向け増税を訴えるなど，かなり現実的な政策路線に徹する選挙運動を展開した．それは，次のような勝利演説に如実に表れていた．

I'm not talking about (6)blind optimism, the kind of hope that just ignores the enormity of the tasks ahead or the road blocks that stand in our path. I'm not talking about (7)the wishful idealism that allows us to just sit on the sidelines or shirk from a fight.…

America, I believe we can build on the progress we've made and continue to fight (8)for new jobs and new opportunities and new security for the middle class. …It doesn't matter whether you're black or white or Hispanic or Asian or Native American or young or old or rich or poor, abled, disabled, gay or straight. You can make it here in America if you're willing to try.

　最後にオバマは，「私たちはこれまでも，そして永遠に諸州が団結したアメリカ」(We are, and forever will be, the United States of America) なのだから，「この国の政治が示すほど私たちは分裂していないので，私はこのような未来をみんな一緒につかめると信じている」(I believe we can seize this future together because we are not as divided as our politics suggests) と，勝利演説を締めくくった．

　ところで，再選を決めた2012年の勝利演説を2008年の初当選時と比較すると，オバマ政権の歩みや姿勢が如実に見えてくる．2つの勝利演説のなかから，使用頻度の高いキーワードを列挙すると次の表のようになる．

2012年の勝利演説

順位	キーワード	回数
1	work	15
2	country	13
3	forward	9
4	future	8
4	hope	8
6	believe	7
6	fight	7
6	thank	7
9	family	5
9	job	5

2008年の勝利演説

順位	キーワード	回数
1	tonight	13
2	people	12
3	nation	8
4	Yes we can	7
5	change	6
5	hope	6
7	answer	5
8	first	4
8	generation	4
10	democracy	3

出典：セレゴ・ジャパン
〈http://japan.internet.com/busnews/20121109/10.html〉

　4年前の勝利演説では，オバマはpeople, nation, hope, democracyなど，アメリカに対する思いや信念を表わす言葉を多用し，Yes we canやchangeによって行動する姿勢を強く訴えた．しかし，再選を決めた勝利演説では，オバマはwork, country, forward, futureなどを多用し，大統領としてなすべき課題がまだ未完であると呼びかけ，国民と共に前進する姿勢を強調した．

　オバマは，再選の勝利演説のなかで，「アメリカにとって最高の日々はこれか

らだ」(for the United States of America, the best is yet to come) と強調したが，失業率は相変わらず危険水域の 7.8％にあり，財政赤字も 2009 年から 1 兆ドルを超える状態が続き，債務不履行（デフォルト）の危機すら払拭されていなかった．それは，2013 年早々に減税停止と歳出削減が重なる「財政の崖」(Fiscal Cliff) への不安が広がっていたためであり，再選を決めた 11 月 7 日，ニューヨーク証券取引所のダウ工業平均株価は急落した．

(2) 2期目就任演説

2013 年 1 月 21 日，ワシントンには約 80 万人が集まり，オバマは 2 期目の就任式に臨んだ．オバマは就任演説のなかで，経済問題の解決に向けて党派を超えた協力を要請し，「私たちは終わりなき旅を続ける」(we continue a never-ending journey) と述べ，今後 4 年間の政権担当に強い意欲を示した．そして，アメリカが次のように試練や危機を乗り越えてきたと訴え，これからも「共に前進する」(move forward together) ことを国民に呼びかけた．

　This generation of Americans has been tested by crises that steeled our resolve and proved our resilience. (9)A decade of war is now ending. An economic recovery has begun. America's possibilities are limitless, …

　For we, the people, understand that our country cannot succeed when a shrinking few do very well and a growing many barely make it. We believe that (10)America's prosperity must rest upon the broad shoulders of a rising middle class.

オバマは，社会保障や財政・医療などの課題を取り上げ，すべての国民が安全と尊厳を手にする権利があると強調した．

　We, the people, still believe that every citizen deserves a basic measure of security and dignity. We must make the hard choices to (11)reduce the cost of health care and the size of our deficit. But we reject the belief that America must choose between caring for the generation that built this country and investing in the generation that will build its future. …

　…We recognize that no matter how responsibly we live our lives, any one of us, at any time, may face a job loss, or a sudden illness, or a home swept away in a terrible storm. The commitments we make to each other – (12)through Medicare, and Medicaid, and Social Security – these things do not sap our initiative; they strengthen us.

　オバマは，アメリカが強い軍隊と法の原則に基づいて同盟国の中心となり，他の国々との紛争を平和的に解決する姿勢を強調した．

We will defend our people and uphold our values through strength of arms and rule of law. We will show the courage to try and (13)resolve our differences with other nations peacefully…. America will remain the anchor of strong alliances in every corner of the globe; and we will renew those institutions that extend our capacity to manage crisis abroad, for (14)no one has a greater stake in a peaceful world than its most powerful nation.

　オバマは，「私たちは，自らのためだけでなく子孫のために，アメリカ人としての責務を果たすべきだ」（We, the people, still believe that our obligations as Americans are not just to ourselves, but to all posterity）と述べ，気候変動の脅威（threat of climate change）に対処し，再生可能エネルギーへの道（path towards sustainable energy sources）を推進することを約束した．そして，最後にオバマは，何度も「私たちの旅は…まで終わらない」（our journey is not complete until…）と未来に賭けるフレーズを繰り返し，「皆さんと私は，市民としてこの国の道筋を決める力を持っている」（You and I, as citizens, have the power to set this country's course）と，国民に呼びかけた．

設問1．下線部（1）〜（4）は，具体的にどのようなことを指していますか．
設問5．下線部（5）は，オバマのどのような姿勢が表れていますか．
設問6．下線部（6）は，どのようなことを指していますか．
設問7．下線部（7）は，どのようなことを指していますか．
設問8．下線部（8）は，具体的に，どのようなことを指していますか．
設問9．下線部（9）は，具体的に，どのようなことを指していますか．
設問10．下線部（10）は，具体的に，どのようなことを指していますか．

設問11. 下線部（11）は，どのようなことを指していますか．
設問12. 下線部（12）は，具体的に，どのようなことを指していますか．
設問13. 下線部（13）は，オバマのどのような姿勢が表れていますか．
設問14. 下線部（14）は，オバマのどのような姿勢が表れていますか．

おわりに

　21世紀のアメリカは，ブッシュとオバマという対照的な大統領のイメージに彩られてきた．それは共和・民主という二大政党の違い，保守対リベラルのイデオロギー対立があり，両極化したアメリカ，分断されたアメリカが格差社会の様相を強めてきたからである．

　しかし，グローバル社会の現実はもっと複雑であり，オバマは，内政・外交両面で妥協や協調を生み出さなければ前進できないことを強く自覚している．アメリカの国民が2度にわたってオバマを大統領に選んだということは，左右の原理主義やイデオロギーよりも価値の多様性を認め，アメリカの単独行動よりも国際協調の姿勢を評価したと言うべきであろう．それは，アメリカの未来に賭けた大きな実験なのかもしれない．

解　答
1. **21世紀のアメリカとオバマの登場**
設問1. 政治的に国民世論を分断し，分裂状態を強めようとする人々がいること．
設問2. アメリカは，政治的にはリベラルや保守など多様な意見があり，人種的には白人，黒人，ヒスパニック，アジア系など多民族社会であるが，アメリカ合衆国は1つである．オバマは，分裂したアメリカをひとつに統合させようとしている．
設問3. ヒスパニックとも呼ばれ，スペイン語を話すメキシコや南米からの移民．
設問4. アメリカ人はひとつの国民であり，全員が星条旗に忠誠を誓い，全員がアメリカ合衆国を守っている．

2. **2008年大統領選挙とオバマ政権の発足**
設問1. 以前より多くのアメリカ人が職を失い，前より少ない給料で働いていること．
設問2. 前より多くのアメリカ人が，車を運転できず，クレジットカードの支払いができず，授

設問 3. 困難な状況に対応できていないのは，ワシントンの政治破綻とブッシュ政権の失政のせいである．
設問 4. ブッシュ政権のもとで，経済が大きく成長したこと．
設問 5. 経済成長率，物価上昇率，国際収支などの，アメリカ経済の基礎的条件が強いこと．
設問 6. 景気後退は心のもち方であること．
設問 7. 低燃費の車をアメリカ国内で製造すること．
設問 8. 風力，太陽光，地熱，バイオ燃料など．
設問 9. 全軍の最高司令官，つまりアメリカ大統領．
設問 10. イラクの政治情勢を安定させ，民主的なイラクを再建すること．
設問 11. テロと核拡散，飢餓やジェノサイド，気候変動や伝染病などに対処するため，21世紀にふさわしい協力関係を世界と構築すること．
設問 12. 当初，大統領候補としては有力ではなく，多くの資金や支援があったわけではなかったこと．
設問 13. まったくの赤の他人に，支持を訴えて戸別訪問をすること．
設問 14. ボランティア組織を作って，何百万という人々が選挙活動に参加したこと．
設問 15. リンカンが，1863年11月19日に行ったゲティスバーグ演説．
設問 16. テロリストなどの暴力と憎悪のネットワークに戦いを挑んでいること．
設問 17. 複雑な金融証券を生み出した，一部の人々の強欲と無責任さが，実体経済とかけ離れ，アメリカ経済を弱体化させたこと．
設問 18. 政府が大きすぎるとか，小さすぎるとかいうことではなく，機能を十分に発揮しているかどうかが大切であること．
設問 19. 国民と政府の間に不可欠な信頼を回復させることが重要であること．
設問 20. 今回の金融危機で，適切な規制や管理がなければ，市場は無軌道で野放図な動きをしてしまうことを思い知らされた．
設問 21. 経済が順調なのは，国内総生産（GDP）の大きさではなく，繁栄が国民にどこまで行き届いているかにかかっている．
設問 22. 核兵器の脅威を減らすこと．
設問 23. テロを起こし，無実の人を惨殺すること．

3. 第1期オバマ政権の実績

設問 1. 世界的な核戦争の脅威は減ったが，核攻撃のリスクは高まった．
設問 2. 核の秘密や核物質が闇市場で取引されている．
設問 3. 核不拡散体制が維持できないところに達するかもしれないこと．

設問 4. 核兵器を使用したことがある唯一の国として，アメリカが核廃絶に向けて行動を起こす道義的責任がある．
設問 5. アメリカが核兵器のない平和で安全な世界を追求すること．
設問 6. アメリカは単独では行動できず，単独では安全を守れないこと．
設問 7. 平和には責任が伴い，犠牲が必然的に伴うこと．
設問 8. オバマケアが今後 10 年間に約 9,000 億ドルの経費がかかる．
設問 9. オバマケアが，現存の医療システムのなかで使われ，浪費されてきた経費で賄うことができる．
設問 10. 長期的には 4 兆ドルもの財政赤字を削減することができる．

4. オバマ再選への道

設問 1. 財政赤字の削減．
設問 2. 税制改革．
設問 3. 移民制度の見直し．
設問 4. 石油依存からの脱却．
設問 5. まだやるべきことがたくさんある．
設問 6. 闇雲な楽観主義．
設問 7. 能天気な理想主義．
設問 8. 中間層のための，新しい仕事，新しい機会，新しい安心．
設問 9. イラク戦争がアメリカ軍の撤兵で終了したこと．
設問 10. アメリカの繁栄は中間層の肩にかかっていること．
設問 11. 医療費と財政赤字の削減．
設問 12. メディケア，メディケイドなどの医療保険，社会保障制度は自発性を奪うものではなく，私たちを強くしてくれるものである．
設問 13. 他の国々との紛争を平和的に解決すること．
設問 14. 世界最強のアメリカほど，平和な世界に貢献できる国はない．

第7章

アメリカの世界観
—— 国家安全保障戦略（NSS）を読む ——

はじめに

　アメリカは世界最大の軍事大国であり，9.11 やイラク戦争以降その単独行動主義が非難されてはいるものの，依然として世界で最も影響力のある国家である．アメリカはいかなる世界観を持ち，自国を含む国際社会全体をどのように捉えているのだろうか．本章ではアメリカの国家安全保障戦略（NSS: National Security Strategy）を読み解きながらアメリカの世界観とその変遷を探っていく．NSSはゴールドウォーター＝ニコルズ国防総省再編法（Goldwater-Nichols Department of Defense Reorganization Act of 1986）によって規定され，大統領が議会に対して，国家安全保障に関わる利益・目標・目的などの指針を説明するための文書である．ジョージ・ブッシュ（George H. W. Bush. 在任 1989-1993 年），ビル・クリントン（Bill Clinton. 在任 1993-2001 年），ジョージ・ブッシュ（George W. Bush. 在任 2001 - 2009 年），バラク・オバマ（Barack Obama. 在任 2009 - 現在）の 4 人の大統領は延べ 13 の NSS を発表している．本章では大統領の文責で執筆された NSS の序文のうち 5 編を取り上げている．安全保障（Security）という言葉の使われ方に注意を払いながら，アメリカの世界観の変遷を理解することが本章のねらいである．各節冒頭には簡単な紹介が付されているので，それらを参考にしながら各節を日本語で要約してみよう．

1. George H. W. Bush, *National Security Strategy of the United States*, (August 1, 1991)

　1989年は衝撃的な1年であった．東欧革命と民主化，東西冷戦の象徴であったベルリンの壁崩壊，米ソ首脳によるマルタ島での冷戦終結宣言．世界構造が大きく変化した．1990年の湾岸戦争では米軍を主力とする多国籍軍がイラク軍を撃破し，超大国アメリカの強さが印象づけられた．こうした秩序変動を踏まえ，NSSは「ポスト冷戦時代」の新しい安全保障概念を提起している．すなわち，ソ連との軍事衝突を想定していた従来の考え方から，より広範な地域紛争に対応すべく新しい世界秩序の中でのアメリカの国際的な役割を打ち出している．安全保障概念が軍事的な側面だけではなく経済的・政治的・社会的な側面へと拡大されている．

A new world order is not a fact; it is an aspiration—and an opportunity. We have within our grasp an extraordinary possibility that few generations have enjoyed—to build a new international system in accordance with our own values and ideals, as old patterns and certainties crumble around us.

　In the Gulf we caught a glimmer of a better future—a new world community brought together by a growing consensus that force cannot be used to settle disputes and that when that consensus is broken, the world will respond. In the Gulf, we saw the United Nations playing the role dreamed of by its founders, with the world's leading nations orchestrating and sanctioning collective action against aggression. But we remain in a period of transition. The old has been swept away, the new not yet fully in place. The obstacles and uncertainties before us are quite real—the daunting problems confronting the hopes for reform in Eastern Europe and the Soviet Union, trade disputes and burdensharing debates among the industrial democracies, and the turmoil and dangers in the developing world.

　Yet, the Gulf crisis showed what the world community is now capable of, and in the very act of meeting that challenge the world community strengthened itself. I hope history will record that the Gulf crisis was the crucible of the new world order.

It is up to us—our generation in America and the world—to bring these extraordinary possibilities to fruition. And in doing this, American leadership is indispensable. That is our challenge.

Our response, outlined in this Report, is shaped by what we are as a people, for our values are the link between our past and our future, between our domestic life and our foreign policy, between our power and our purpose. It is our deepest belief that all nations and peoples seek political and economic freedom; that governments must rest their rightful authority on the consent of the governed, and must live in peace with their neighbors. The collapse of the Communist idea has shown that our vision of individual rights—a vision imbedded in the faith of our Founders—speaks to humanity's enduring hopes and aspirations.

Official portrait of President George H. W. Bush, Oval Office of the White House, Washington, DC, February 15, 1989, George Bush Presidential Library and Museum, Photo ID: P00565

It is this abiding faith in democracy that steels us to deal with a world that, for all our hope, remains a dangerous place—a world of ethnic antagonisms, national rivalries, religious tensions, spreading weaponry, personal ambitions and lingering authoritarianism. For America, there can be no retreat from the world's problems. Within the broader community of nations, we see our own role clearly. We must not only protect our citizens and our interests, but help create a new world in which our fundamental values not only survive but flourish. We must work with others, but we must also be a leader.

2. Bill Clinton, *A National Security Strategy of Engagement and Enlargement*, (July 1, 1994)

クリントン政権における最初のNSSである．ポスト冷戦期における国際環境の変化やそこにおけるアメリカの新しい役割を定義するという方向性はブッシュ政権と大きく変わらない．ただし，ブッシュ政権時代のNSSにおいては示唆されるにとどまっていた安全保障概念の拡大が明確に意識されている．国民や領土と並んでアメリカの生活様式（our way of life）が安全保障の対象として述べられ，狭義の軍事問題だけではなく，経済の活性化や民主主義の促進までもがその目標として掲げられている．

Protecting our nation's security—our people, our territory and our way of life— is my Administration's foremost mission and constitutional duty. The end of the Cold War fundamentally changed America's security imperatives. The central security challenge of the past half century—the threat of communist expansion—is gone. The dangers we face today are more diverse. Ethnic conflict is spreading and rogue states pose a serious danger to regional stability in many corners of the globe. The proliferation of weapons of mass destruction represents a major challenge to our security. Large scale environmental degradation, exacerbated by rapid population growth, threatens to undermine political stability in many countries and regions.

At the same time, we have unparalleled opportunities to make our

Courtesy, William J. Clinton Presidential Library, Photo ID: P78150_21

nation safer and more prosperous. Our military might is unparalleled. We now have a truly global economy linked by an instantaneous communications network, which offers growing scope for American jobs and American investment. The community of democratic nations is growing, enhancing the prospects for political stability, peaceful conflict resolution and greater dignity and hope for the people of the world. The international community is beginning to act together to address pressing global environmental needs.

Never has American leadership been more essential—to navigate the shoals of the world's new dangers and to capitalize on its opportunities. American assets are unique: our military strength, our dynamic economy, our powerful ideals and, above all, our people. We can and must make the difference through our engagement; but our involvement must be carefully tailored to serve our interests and priorities.

This report, submitted in accordance with Section 603 of the Goldwater-Nichols Defense Department Reorganization Act of 1986, elaborates a new national security strategy for this new era. Focussing on new threats and new opportunities, its central goats are:

- To credibly sustain our security with military forces that are ready to fight.
- To bolster America's economic revitalization.
- To promote democracy abroad.

Over the past seventeen months, my Administration has worked to pursue these goals. This national security strategy report presents the strategy that has guided this effort. It is premised on a belief that the line between our domestic and foreign policies has increasingly disappeared—that we must revitalize our economy if we are to sustain our military forces, foreign initiatives and global influence, and that we must engage actively abroad if we are to open foreign markets and create jobs for our people.

We believe that our goals of enhancing our security, bolstering our economic prosperity, and promoting democracy are mutually supportive. Secure nations are more likely to support free trade and maintain democratic structures. Nations with growing economies and strong trade ties are more likely to feel secure and to work toward freedom. And democratic states are less likely to threaten our interests and more likely to cooperate with the U.S. to meet security threats and promote sustainable development.

Since my Administration began, we have taken actions to meet these goals. To enhance global security, for example, we have pursued peace initiatives in the Middle East, established NATO's Partnership for Peace, reached a denuclearization agreement with Ukraine and Russia and implemented a firm strategy for a non-nuclear Korean peninsula. To bolster prosperity at home and around the world, we have passed the North American Free Trade Agreement, worked to open Asian-Pacific markets through the first-ever summit meeting of the Organization for Asian Pacific Economic Cooperation, lowered export controls and—having successfully completed the seventh GATT round—will now work with Congress to pass it this year. Our actions to promote democracy include our support for South Africa's recent transformation, aid to a new democratic Russia and Central and Eastern European nations, and our work with our Western Hemisphere neighbors, which will culminate at December's Summit of the Americas.

Even with the Cold War over, our nation must maintain military forces that are sufficient to deter diverse threats and, when necessary, to fight and win against our adversaries. While many factors ultimately contribute to our nation's safety and well-being, no single component is more important than the men and women who wear America's uniform and stand sentry over our security. Their skill, service and dedication constitute the core of our defenses. Today our military is the best-equipped, best-trained and best-prepared fighting force in the *world*, and I am committed to ensure that it remains so.

Our national security strategy reflects both America's interests and our values. Our commitment to freedom, equality and human dignity continues to serve as a beacon of hope to peoples around the world. The vitality, creativity and diversity of American society are important sources of national strength in a global economy that is dynamic, multi-cultural and increasingly driven by ideas and information.

Our prospects in this new era are promising. The specter of nuclear annihilation has dramatically receded. The historic events of the past year—including the handshake between Israel and the PLO and the breakthroughs by Nelson Mandela and F.W. DeKlerk that culminated in the election of a multi-racial parliament and a government headed by President Mandela—suggest this era's possibilities for progress toward security, prosperity and democracy.

Our nation can only address this era's dangers and opportunities if we remain actively engaged in global affairs. We are the world's greatest power, and we have global interests as well as responsibilities. As our nation learned after World War I, we can find no security for America in isolationism, nor prosperity in protectionism. For the American people to be safer and enjoy expanding opportunities, our nation must work to deter would-be aggressors, open foreign markets, promote the spread of democracy abroad, encourage sustainable development and pursue new opportunities for peace.

Our national security requires the patient application of American will and resources. We can only sustain that necessary investment with the broad, bipartisan support of the American people and their representatives in Congress. The full participation of Congress is essential to the success of our new engagement, and I will consult with Congress at every step of the policy making and implementation process. The Cold War may be over, but the need for American leadership abroad remains as strong as ever. I am committed to building a new public consensus to sustain our active engagement abroad. This document is a part of that commitment.

3. Bill Clinton, *A National Security Strategy for a Global Age*, (December 1, 2000).

21世紀に向けての新たな秩序の構築を模索している．一方では世界経済や国際機関を通じたグローバルな一体性や連帯を強調し，他方ではグローバル化のもたらす未曾有の脅威（核拡散，生物・化学兵器，テロ，国際犯罪）を論じている．その上で，自由と民主主義という価値を共有する世界の国々との協調を謳っている．

As we enter the new millennium, we are blessed to be citizens of a country enjoying record prosperity, with no deep divisions at home, no overriding external threats abroad, and history's most powerful military ready to defend our interests around the world. Americans of earlier eras may have hoped one day to live in a nation that could claim just one of these blessings. Probably few expected to experience them all; fewer still all at once.

Our success is cause for pride in what we've done, and gratitude for what we have inherited. But the most important matter is what we now make of this moment. Some may be tempted to believe that open markets and societies will inevitably spread in an era of expanding global trade and communications, or assume that our wealth and power alone will protect us from the troubles of the outside world. But that approach falls for the old myth of an "outside" world, and ignores the defining features of our age: the rise of interdependence. More than ever, prosperity and security in America depend on prosperity and security around the globe. In this age, America can advance its interests and ideals only by leading efforts to meet common challenges. We must deploy America's financial, diplomatic and military resources to stand up for peace and security, promote global prosperity, and advance democracy and human rights around the world.

This demands strengthening our alliances with Europe and Asia, and adapting them to meet emerging challenges. Our alliances in Europe and Asia are stronger because they are organized to advance a permanent set of shared interests, rather than to defeat a single threat. We must continue working with our allies towards a peaceful, democratic, undivided Europe, with NATO as a deterrent to new conflict and a magnet for new democracies. In Asia, we must build on strategic alliance with Japan to define new approaches to post-Cold War threats. And, we must enhance cooperation with South Korea as we encourage North Korea's emergence from isolation and continue to diminish the missile threat.

Just as we strengthen our alliances, we must build principled, constructive, clear-eyed relations with our former adversaries Russia and China. We must be mindful of threats to peace while also maximizing chances that both Russia and China move toward greater internal openness, stability and prosperity, seizing on the desire of both countries to participate in the global economy and global institutions, insisting that both accept the obligations as well as the benefits of integration. With Russia, that means continuing our work to reduce the nuclear danger, to assure strategic stability, and to define its future role in Europe, while supporting the emergence of democratic institutions and the rule of law. With China, that means continuing to press for adherence to nonproliferation standards and peaceful dialogue with Taiwan, while holding Chinese leaders to the conditions of entry into the WTO, which offer the best hope of internal reform.

To protect the peace and promote security, we must work to resolve conflicts before they escalate and harm vital U.S. interests. In the 1990s, the United States has been actively engaged in seeking peace in the Middle East, in the Balkans, between Greece and Turkey, between India and Pakistan, in Northern Ireland, between Peru and Ecuador, and Eritrea and Ethiopia. These efforts, undertaken in partnership with friends and allies, help to avert wider conflicts that might endanger global stability, ease humanitarian catastrophes, while adding moral authority to America's might in the world. American overwhelming power and influence is far less likely to breed resentment if it is used to advance the cause of peace.

We also must identify and address new national security challenges, accentuated by new technology and open borders. We have identified a new security agenda that addresses contemporary threats such as the proliferation of nuclear, chemical and biological weapons, terrorism, and international crime. New efforts must continue to build on initiatives such as the extension of the Nonproliferation Treaty, the containment of nations seeking to acquire and use weapons of mass destruction, increased antiterrorism cooperation, stepped up efforts to combat trafficking in drugs, arms, and human- beings, and our first-ever national strategy for cybersecurity. Our new security agenda recognizes that in a global age, threats to America do not simply come from determined enemies and deadly weapons. Our efforts to curb global warming through the Kyoto protocol are vital to protect America from a future of rising sea levels and economic disruption. Our leadership in the international fight against infectious diseases, especially HIV/AIDS, is critical to defeat a threat that kills massively, crosses frontiers and destabilizes whole regions.

Finally, there can be no security where there is no hope of prosperity. We must continue to promote the spread of global markets in ways that advance economic growth, honor our values, and help alleviate economic disparity. We must build on the creation of the WTO, and of NAFTA, on the passage of PNTR for China, on extending trade preferences to nations in Africa and the Caribbean Basin, and on the nearly 300 trade agreements we have signed that have contributed to the longest U.S. economic expansion in history. At the same time, we must understand that trade, by itself, is not enough to lift the most desperate nations out of poverty or prevent the world from becoming bitterly divided between haves and have nots. That's why we have led in promoting the HIPC initiative to provide deeper debt reduction for countries with unsustainable debt burdens, and placed global development issues at the forefront of the international agenda.

More than 50 years ago, Harry Truman said: "We are in a position now of making the world safe for democracy, if we don't crawl in a shell and act selfish and foolish." He believed that in the wake of our triumph in World War 11, America had the ability and a responsibility to shape world events, so that we would not be shaped by them. Truman was right, and the historical forces he saw then have only intensified since the Cold War.

The ability to assure global security, shared prosperity and freedom is beyond the power of any one nation. But the actions of many nations often follow from the actions of one. America today has power and authority never seen before in the history of the world. We must continue use it, in partnership with those who share our values, to seize the opportunities and meet the challenges of a global age.

4. George W. Bush, *The National Security Strategy of the United States*, (September 17, 2002).

9.11以降に推し進められた「テロとの戦争（War on Terrorism）」を肯定するブッシュ・ドクトリンである．自由と全体主義との戦いとして20世紀を振り返り，自由と民主主義を擁護し，テロリストや独裁者たちと戦うことが平和を追求する手段であると提起している．アメリカが戦うのは自国の利益のためではなく，民主主義・自由市場・自由貿易など世界にとってかけがえのない価値を守るためであるという．ブッシュ・ドクトリンは「テロとの戦争」など急進的な内容を含むものだが，こうした論理自体はクリントン政権期から見られるものである．むしろ政治的価値に対しての期待が順次拡大し，「テロとの戦争」によってそれが頂点に達したと考えられる．

The great struggles of the twentieth century between liberty and totalitarianism ended with a decisive victory for the forces of freedom—and a single sustainable model for national success: freedom, democracy, and free enterprise.

Standing on top of a crumpled fire truck with retired New York City firefighter Bob Beckwith, President George W. Bush rallies firefighters and rescue workers Friday, September 14, 2001, during an impromptu speech at the site of the collapsed World Trade Center towers. "I can hear you," President Bush said. "The rest of the world hears you. And the people who knocked these buildings down will hear all of us soon." (Courtesy George W. Bush Presidential Library and Museum. Photo ID: P7365-23A).

In the twenty-first century, only nations that share a commitment to protecting basic human rights and guaranteeing political and

economic freedom will be able to unleash the potential of their people and assure their future prosperity. People everywhere want to be able to speak freely; choose who will govern them; worship as they please; educate their children—male and female; own property; and enjoy the benefits of their labor. These values of freedom are right and true for every person, in every society— and the duty of protecting these values against their enemies is the common calling of freedom-loving people across the globe and across the ages.

Today, the United States enjoys a position of unparalleled military strength and great economic and political influence. In keeping with our heritage and principles, we do not use our strength to press for unilateral advantage. We seek instead to create a balance of power that favors human freedom: conditions in which all nations and all societies can choose for themselves the rewards and challenges of political and economic liberty. In a world that is safe, people will be able to make their own lives better. We will defend the peace by fighting terrorists and tyrants. We will preserve the peace by building good relations among the great powers. We will extend the peace by encouraging free and open societies on every continent.

Defending our Nation against its enemies is the first and fundamental commitment of the Federal Government. Today, that task has changed dramatically. Enemies in the past needed great armies and great industrial capabilities to endanger America. Now, shadowy networks of individuals can bring great chaos and suffering to our shores for less than it costs to purchase a single tank. Terrorists are organized to penetrate open societies and to turn the power of modern technologies against us.

To defeat this threat we must make use of every tool in our arsenal—military power, better homeland defenses, law enforcement, intelligence, and vigorous efforts to cut off terrorist financing. The war against terrorists of global reach is a global enterprise of uncertain duration. America will help nations that need our assistance in combating terror. And America will hold to account nations that are compromised by terror, including those who harbor terrorists—because the allies of terror are the enemies of civilization. The United States and countries cooperating with us must not allow the terrorists to develop new home bases. Together, we will seek to deny them sanctuary at every turn.

The gravest danger our Nation faces lies at the crossroads of radicalism and technology. Our enemies have openly declared that they are seeking weapons of mass destruction, and evidence indicates that they are doing so with determination. The United States will not allow these efforts to succeed. We will build defenses against ballistic missiles and other means of delivery. We will cooperate with other nations to deny, contain, and curtail our enemies' efforts to acquire dangerous technologies. And, as a matter of common sense and self-defense, America will act against such emerging threats before they are fully formed. We cannot defend America and our friends by hoping for the best. So we must be prepared to defeat our enemies' plans, using the best intelligence and proceeding with deliberation. History will judge harshly those who saw this coming danger but failed to act. In the new world we have entered, the only path to peace and security is the path of action.

As we defend the peace, we will also take advantage of an historic opportunity to preserve the peace. Today, the international community has the best chance since the rise of the nation-state in the seventeenth century to build a world where great powers compete in peace instead of continually prepare for war. Today, the world's great powers find ourselves on the same side—united by common dangers of terrorist violence and chaos. The United States will build on these common interests to promote global security. We are also increasingly united by common values. Russia is in the midst of a hopeful transition, reaching for its democratic future and a partner in the war on terror. Chinese leaders are discovering that economic freedom is the only source of national wealth. In time, they will find that social and political freedom is the only source of national greatness. America will encourage the advancement of democracy and economic openness in both nations, because these are the best foundations for domestic stability and international order. We will strongly resist aggression from other great powers—even as we welcome their peaceful pursuit of prosperity, trade, and cultural advancement.

Finally, the United States will use this moment of opportunity to extend the benefits of freedom across the globe. We will actively work to bring the hope of democracy, development, free markets, and free trade to every corner of the world. The events of September 11, 2001, taught us that weak states, like Afghanistan, can pose as great a danger to our national interests as strong states.

Poverty does not make poor people into terrorists and murderers. Yet poverty, weak institutions, and corruption can make weak states vulnerable to terrorist networks and drug cartels within their borders.

The United States will stand beside any nation determined to build a better future by seeking the rewards of liberty for its people. Free trade and free markets have proven their ability to lift whole societies out of poverty—so the United States will work with individual nations, entire regions, and the entire global trading community to build a world that trades in freedom and therefore grows in prosperity. The United States will deliver greater development assistance through the New Millennium Challenge Account to nations that govern justly, invest in their people, and encourage economic freedom. We will also continue to lead the world in efforts to reduce the terrible toll of HIV/AIDS and other infectious diseases.

In building a balance of power that favors freedom, the United States is guided by the conviction that all nations have important responsibilities. Nations that enjoy freedom must actively fight terror. Nations that depend on international stability must help prevent the spread of weapons of mass destruction. Nations that seek international aid must govern themselves wisely, so that aid is well spent. For freedom to thrive, accountability must be expected and required.

We are also guided by the conviction that no nation can build a safer, better world alone. Alliances and multilateral institutions can multiply the strength of freedom-loving nations. The United States is committed to lasting institutions like the United Nations, the World Trade Organization, the Organization of American States, and NATO as well as other long-standing alliances. Coalitions of the willing can augment these permanent institutions. In all cases, international obligations are to be taken seriously. They are not to be undertaken symbolically to rally support for an ideal without furthering its attainment.

Freedom is the non-negotiable demand of human dignity; the birthright of every person—in every civilization. Throughout history, freedom has been threatened by war and terror; it has been challenged by the clashing wills of powerful states and the evil designs of tyrants; and it has been tested by widespread poverty and disease. Today, humanity holds in its hands the opportunity to further freedom's triumph over all these foes. The United States welcomes our responsibility to lead in this great mission.

5. Barack Obama, *National Security Strategy*, (May 27, 2010).

　オバマ政権のNSSにはブッシュ政権時と比べて際立った特徴がある．経済政策の重視と多国間主義の強調である．一方で，自由や市場経済，社会発展などの価値が称揚され国家安全保障における経済政策の重要度が高まっている．他方で多国間主義に基づいた国際協調が重視され，テロリズムに対しての多国間主義のアプローチが唱導されるなど，ブッシュ政権と比べるとアプローチがかなり穏健化している．

Time and again in our Nation's history, Americans have risen to meet- and to shape moments of transition. This must be one of those moments. We live in a time of sweeping change. The success of free nations, open markets, and social progress in recent decades has accelerated globalization on an unprecedented scale. This has opened the doors of opportunity around the globe, extended democracy to hundreds of millions of people, and made peace possible among the major powers. Yet globalization has also intensified the dangers we face from international terrorism and the spread of deadly technologies, to economic upheaval and a changing climate.

　For nearly a decade, our Nation has been at war with a far-reaching network of violence and hatred. Even as we end one war in Iraq, our military has been called upon to renew our focus on Afghanistan as part of a commitment to disrupt, dismantle, and defeat al-Qa'ida and its affiliates. This is part of a broad, multinational effort that is right and just, and we will be unwavering in our commitment to the security of our people, allies, and partners, Moreover, as we face multiple threats from nations, nonstate actors, and failed states we will maintain the military superiority that has secured our country, and underpinned global security, for decades.

Yet as we fight the wars in front of us, we must see the horizon beyond them a world in which America is stronger, more secure, and is able to overcome our challenges while appealing to the aspirations of people around the world. To get there, we must pursue a strategy of national renewal and global leadership a strategy that rebuilds the foundation of American strength and influence.

http://www.whitehouse.gov/administration/president-obama (last accessed, May 4, 2013.)

Our strategy starts by recognizing that our strength and influence abroad begins with the steps we take at home. We must grow our economy and reduce our deficit. We must educate our children to compete in an age where knowledge is capital, and the marketplace is global. We must develop the clean energy that can power new industry, unbind us from foreign oil, and preserve our planet. We must pursue science and research that enables discovery, and unlocks wonders as unforeseen to us today as the surface of the moon and the microchip were a century ago. Simply put, we must see American innovation as a foundation of American power.

We must also build and integrate the capabilities that can advance our interests, and the interests we share with other countries and peoples. Our Armed Forces will always be a cornerstone of our security, but they must be complemented. Our security also depends upon diplomats who can act in every corner of the world, from grand capitals to dangerous outposts; development experts who can strengthen governance and support human dignity; and intelligence and law enforcement that can unravel plots, strengthen justice systems, and work seamlessly with other countries.

The burdens of a young century cannot fall on American shoulders alone indeed, our adversaries would like to see America sap our strength by overextending our power. In the past, we have had the foresight to act judiciously and to avoid acting alone. We were part of the most powerful wartime coalition in human history through World War II, and stitched together a community of free nations and institutions to endure a Cold War. We are clear—eyed about the challenge of mobilizing collective action, and the shortfalls of our international system. But America has not succeeded by stepping outside the currents of international cooperation. We have succeeded by steering those currents in the direction of liberty and justice so that nations thrive by meeting their responsibilities and face consequences when they don't.

To do so, we will be steadfast in strengthening those old alliances that have served us so well, while modernizing them to meet the challenges of a new century. As influence extends to more countries and capitals, we will build new and deeper partnerships in every region, and strengthen international standards and institutions. This engagement is no end in itself. The international order we seek is one that can resolve the challenges of our times countering violent extremism and insurgency; stopping the spread of nuclear weapons and securing nuclear materials; combating a changing climate and sustaining global growth; helping countries feed themselves and care for their sick; resolving and preventing conflict, while also healing its wounds.

In all that we do, we will advocate for and advance the basic rights upon which our Nation was founded, and which peoples of every race and region have made their own. We promote these values by living them, including our commitment to the rule of law. We will strengthen international norms that protect these rights, and create space and support for those who resist repression. Our commitment to human dignity includes support for development, which is why we will fight poverty and corruption. And we reject the notion that lasting security and prosperity can be found by turning away from universal rights democracy does not merely represent our better angels, it stands in opposition to aggression and injustice, and our support for universal rights is both fundamental to American leadership and a source of our strength in the world.

As a Nation made up of people from every race, region, faith, and culture, America will persist in promoting peace among different peoples and believes that democracy and individual empowerment need not come at the expense of cherished identities. Indeed, no nation should be better positioned to lead in an era of globalization than America the Nation that helped bring globalization about, whose institutions are designed to prepare individuals to succeed in a competitive world, and whose people trace their roots to every country on the face of the Earth.

As a citizen, Senator, and President, I have always believed that America's greatest asset is its people from the awe I felt as a child watching a space capsule pulled out of the Pacific, to the strength I drew from workers rebuilding their lives in Illinois, to the respect that I have for the generation of Americans who serve our country today. That is why I also believe that we must foster even deeper connections among Americans and peoples around the globe. Our long-term security will come not from our ability to instill fear in other peoples, but through our capacity to speak to their hopes, And that work will best be done through the power of the decency and dignity of the American people our troops and diplomats, but also our private sector, nongovernmental organizations, and citizens. All of us have a role to play.

From the birth of our liberty, America has had a faith in the future a belief that where we're going is better than where we've been, even when the path ahead is uncertain. To fulfill that promise, generations of Americans have built upon the foundation of our forefathers finding opportunity, fighting injustice, and forging a more perfect Union. We have also created webs of commerce, supported an international architecture of laws and institutions, and spilled American blood in foreign lands not to build an empire, but to shape a world in which more individuals and nations could determine their own destiny, and live with the peace and dignity that they deserve.

In 2010, America is hardened by wars, and inspired by the servicemen and women who fight them. We are disciplined by a devastating economic crisis, and determined to see that its legacy is a new foundation for prosperity; and we are bound by a creed that has guided us at home, and served as a beacon to the world, America's greatness is not assured each generation's place in history is a question unanswered. But even as we are tested by new challenges, the question of our future is not one that will be answered for us, it is one that will be answered by us. And in a young century whose trajectory is uncertain, America is ready to lead once more.

おわりに

　ポスト冷戦期におけるアメリカのNSSの展開を検討した．アメリカの世界観の変化には「安全保障」をどのように捉えるのかという根本的な視座の転換が反映されている．冷戦時代には軍事的な問題として理解されていた国家安全保障が，冷戦構造の崩壊によって脅威が拡散し，経済問題や社会問題，自由と民主主義，アメリカ的生活様式などの政治的価値の追求までもが安全保障の主たる対象としてリスト化されている．その後，9.11のテロ以降は「テロとの戦争」の名の下に「自由と民主主義」といった政治的価値の追求が安全保障概念の基調となる．オバマ政権以降こうした傾向は緩和されているが，他方で経済問題についての比重は高まっている．つまり，ポスト冷戦期におけるアメリカの世界観の変化とは，冷戦構造の崩壊という国際社会の秩序変動を踏まえ，その新しい秩序の中

で自国の安全保障に対する概念が，軍事的な問題から経済・社会・政治・価値観へと拡大していく過程である．政権担当者がそれぞれどのような価値を重視して外交政策や安全保障政策を推し進めてきたのかを検討することは，アメリカ政治やその世界観を理解する上で重要な課題であろう．

第8章

日米の文化学術交流
── 太平洋の架け橋を志した新渡戸稲造 ──

はじめに

　幕末生まれの新渡戸稲造は、太平洋を何度も往復し、日米の相互理解に尽くしました。以下の文章を読んで、新渡戸をめぐる次の五点を、日本語または英語でまとめてみましょう。①米国留学で何を学んだか。②なぜ米国で『武士道』を出版したか。③日米交換教授の務めから何を自覚したか。④晩年の渡米の目的は何か。⑤米国をどう見ていたか。これらのポイントは、新渡戸の取り組みを考えていく手がかりになるでしょう。

1. アメリカとの出会い

　The Japanese peacebuilder Inazo Nitobe devoted his whole life to promoting international cooperation, and achieved some peaceful objectives for his own country and the United States (U.S.) as well as the world community.

　Starting with the publication of *Bushido: The Soul of Japan* in the U.S., Nitobe played an active part in bridging the gap between Eastern culture and Western culture. Nitobe's initiatives influenced cultural and academic cooperation between Japan and the U.S. They include the activities of the professor exchange program of the Carnegie Endowment for International Peace; service to the League of Nations; delegations of the Institute of Pacific Relations; citizen diplomacy in the critical situation after the Manchurian Incident; and the practice of international journalism through the serial publication "Editorial Jottings." Nitobe's career overlapped with Japan's process of modernization, and his endeavors represent the building of mutual relationships between modernizing Japan and modernized America.

　As you can see in Table 1, encountering America was crucially important

Table 1: A Sketch of Inazo Nitobe's Life

Year	Major Event
1862	Born in Morioka
1877	Studies at Sapporo Agricultural College
1883	Studies at Tokyo University
1884	Studies at Johns Hopkins University, Baltimore, the U.S.
1886	Joins the Society of Friends in Baltimore as the first Japanese member
1887	Studies at Bonn University, Germany (later, studies at University of Halle and University of Berlin)
1891	Marries Mary Elkinton in Philadelphia, the U.S., and becomes a professor at Sapporo Agricultural College
1892	Loses his first son soon after birth
1900	Publishes *Bushido: The Soul of Japan* in Philadelphia
1901	Becomes an agricultural engineer for the Governor-General of Taiwan, and works for the development of sugar production
1903	Becomes a professor at Kyoto Imperial University
1906	Becomes the principal of the First High School and a professor at Tokyo Imperial University
1911	Visits the U.S. on a lecture tour as Carnegie Endowment for International Peace Program's first Japanese exchange professor
1918	Becomes the first president of Tokyo Women's University
1920	Becomes the first Japanese Under-Secretary General of the League of Nations in Geneva, Switzerland
1922	Helps establish the International Committee on Intellectual Cooperation under the League of Nations
1929	Becomes Chief Director of the Institute of Pacific Relations, represents Japan at the Pacific Conference in Kyoto, and becomes an advisory editor of the English dailies, *Osaka Mainichi* and *Tokyo Nichi Nichi*
1931	Represents Japan at the Pacific Conference in Shanghai, China
1932	Visits the U.S. on a lecture tour as a private citizen to ease people's anti-Japan feelings after the Manchurian Incident
1933	Represents Japan at the Pacific Conference in Banff, Canada, and passes away after the conference in Victoria

©2013 Maki Taniguchi

for Nitobe's life. Nitobe was born into a samurai family in Morioka in 1862, when the Tokugawa regime was coming to an end. It had been nine years since Matthew Calbraith Perry (1794-1858), Commodore of the U.S. Navy, had urged Japan to open itself to the world in 1853. Nitobe grew up in the period of transition from old feudal Japan to new democratic Japan.

Nitobe's education at Sapporo Agricultural College as a second generation student deeply impacted him. Since vice president William Smith Clark (1826-86) taught only the first generation students, Nitobe could not be under Clark's tutelage. (Clark came to Sapporo, while he was on leave from the presidency of Massachusetts Agricultural College, now University of Massachusetts Amherst, just for eight months.) However, Clark's educational principles of character-building based on Christianity were inherited by the educational policies for the second generation students. At this boarding school, students followed the Western way of life, having western meals and wearing Western uniforms. Lessons were taught in English by teachers from the U.S. Above all, each student was provided with a Bible. Through this Christian-based education, Nitobe came to open himself to the Western world, especially to the U.S. His Sapporo days gradually aroused admiration for American culture.

In 1883, Nitobe continued his education at Tokyo University. Before entering the university, Nitobe had an interview with the Dean of Faculty. In the interview, Nitobe told the dean that he wanted to take English literature for his minor, to be a bridge across the Pacific Ocean. Here, Nitobe expressed his determination to make every effort to foster cross-cultural understanding between the East and the West.

In fact, Nitobe carved out a career for himself in the U.S. He started studying at Johns Hopkins University, Baltimore in 1884. In one seminar on international relations, Nitobe worked with a classmate, who later became the U.S. president Thomas Woodrow Wilson (1856-1924). Nitobe's encounter with America involved not only absorbing academic studies and advanced civilization but also people's ways of thinking and sophisticated culture. He was inspired by people's respect for individuality and independency.

During the stay in the U.S., Nitobe had an insight into American civilization and culture. He learned that recognition of people's dignity was the base of American democracy. It was eye-opening for him to appreciate the sense of personality. Even in the Meiji era, many Japanese people's interactions still depended on social authority rather than individuality. It was so deeply engraved in Nitobe' mind that he advocated the value of individuals all his life to awaken Japanese people's sense of personality.

Moreover, Nitobe's religious life was enriched in America. While studying at Johns Hopkins University, Nitobe became the first Japanese Quaker in 1886. The central teaching of the Religious Society of Friends, whose members are known as Quakers, is to believe in each individual's God-given "inner light" or "seed" regardless of their race, religion, gender, or social status. The Quaker belief that all are created equal by God strengthened Nitobe's respect for human equality even further. He lived up to this essential tenet of Quakerism acknowledging God's presence within himself, and believed Quakerism to be the right vessel for integrating his two different identities as Japanese and a Christian.

Through Quaker meetings, Nitobe found a spiritual partner, Mary Patterson Elkinton (1857-1938), and ultimately married her. Though Nitobe and Mary shared the same faith, there were strong oppositions to their marriage from the Elkintons. The *New York Times* (on January 2, 1891) reported the Quaker union, and it read that every effort was made in advance to prevent their marriage. There seems to have been insurmountable barriers of intercultural and interracial feelings between Japan and the U.S. at that time. Nitobe and Mary's relationship was a microcosm of Japan-U.S. relations. Nitobe felt that it was his mission to build mutual trust inside and outside his home.

This is how Nitobe's desire to become a bridge across the Pacific Ocean led to his studying abroad in the U.S. In his later years (on April 2, 1929), Nitobe looked back on how the ambition in youth guided to peace activism throughout his life in an article of the Japanese English newspaper, *Osaka Mainichi*, as follows:

> This dream of ardent youth proved to be the guiding motive in accepting a post in the international secretariat at Geneva, and a constant incentive in my seven years of service there. Nor has that ideal been in the least dimmed as I now join the Osaka Mainichi and the Tokyo Nichi Nichi as Adviser, charged with what I conceive as a pleasant task, of writing and working for its English edition. (*Nitobe Inazo Zenshu*. Vol.23, p.254.)

Thus began Nitobe's long journey to intercultural cooperation, and the following sections will chronologically trace his path in more detail.

2. アメリカでの『武士道』出版

Nitobe's lifework of cultivating understanding between Japan and America first took shape in his publishing of *Bushido: The Soul of Japan*. It was published in Philadelphia, the U.S. (by the Leeds & Biddle Co. Printers and Publishers) in 1900, and reimported to Japan later. Nitobe completed the English masterpiece, while he was recovering from illness in Monterey. Bushido is the ethical codes of bushi who belonged to the warrior class in the Japanese feudal era, and it essentially valued social authority rather than each individual's personality.

Nitobe wrote *Bushido* in English, because he targeted readers of Western people. Incidentally, Nitobe is considered to be one of the three masters of English writing in Japan, along with Kanzo Uchimura (Christian writer, 1861-1930) and Tenshin Okakura (art curator, 1863-1913). Nitobe especially tried to

第 8 章　日米の文化学術交流　──　太平洋の架け橋を志した新渡戸稲造　──　*167*

Table 2: Contents of Nitobe's *Bushido: The Soul of Japan*

Structure	Content
Chapter 1: Introduction	Definition of bushido
Chapter 2: Introduction	Origins of bushido
Chapter 3: Commentary	Notions of justice
Chapter 4: Commentary	Notions of courage
Chapter 5: Commentary	Notions of benevolence
Chapter 6: Commentary	Notions of politeness
Chapter 7: Commentary	Notions of sincerity
Chapter 8: Commentary	Notions of honor
Chapter 9: Commentary	Notions of loyalty
Chapter 10: Commentary	Bushido and education
Chapter 11: Commentary	Bushido and self-control
Chapter 12: Commentary	Bushido and self-disembowelment
Chapter 13: Commentary	Bushido and the sword
Chapter 14: Commentary	Bushido and women
Chapter 15: Discussion	Impacts of bushido
Chapter 16: Discussion	Bushido in modern society
Chapter 17: Discussion	Bushido in future society

©2013 Maki Taniguchi

appeal to people in the U.S. The purpose of this work was to show how unique traditions Japanese culture embraced. In those days, Japan was regarded as an underdeveloped country, both economically and culturally, among the Great Powers. Nitobe's agenda was to make Western people acknowledge Japan's profound culture. As Table 2 indicates, in *Bushido*, Nitobe eloquently introduces traditional virtues of bushido to readers overseas by quoting from European literature, and discusses the possibility of transformation of the old ethical codes in the future.

To Nitobe's delight, *Bushido* was favorably accepted in the U.S. Many book-review columns in such papers as *American, Inquirer*, and *Record*, commended it as a work of great English literature. Among those, the review by

Julian Hawthorne (1846-1934), son of Nathaniel Hawthorne (novelist, 1804-64) was conspicuous. This critic highly praised the piece, stating that Nitobe made the East known to the West with extensive knowledge quite on a par with Western people.

In this way, Nitobe's *Bushido* took a leading part in promoting cross-cultural understanding for American people, most of whom had known only about seppuku or hara-kiri (stomach-cutting), talking of Japanese bushi. Nitobe felt exceedingly honored when one of the readers of the book, U.S. President Theodore Roosevelt (1858-1919), appreciated the moral principles of bushido and bought some copies to distribute them to his friends and family. To some extent, Nitobe succeeded in deepening people's understanding about the essence of Japanese culture.

It should be noted that Nitobe's *Bushido* is not a past-oriented specimen of old values but a future-oriented guide for the transformation of those values. The following descriptions in the work demonstrate Nitobe's vision for the future of bushido morals.

> Callings nobler and broader than a warrior's claim our attention to-day. With an enlarged view of life, with the growth of democracy, with better knowledge of other peoples and nations, the Confucian idea of benevolence—dare I also add the Buddhist idea of pity?—will expand into the Christian conception of love. Men have become more than subjects, having grown to the estate of citizens; nay, they are more than citizens—being men. (*Nitobe Inazo Zenshu*. Vol.12, p.137.)

Nitobe explored a post-bushido approach toward creating an ethical code based on people's own conscience, not authority.

According to Nitobe, the codes of bushido needed to be transformed in accordance with the diversification of people's ways of thinking. In *Bushido*, Nitobe suggests that Christianity should be grafted onto traditional bushido to build a new value system in Japan, from the viewpoint of a Japanese Christian.

It seems that Nitobe's argument coincided with his own process of integrating his identity as Japanese with his identity as a Christian.

On one hand, Nitobe aimed to show Western people Japanese people's senses of morality grounded on bushido, which he considered as preparation for acceptance of Christianity in Japan. On the other hand, Nitobe foresaw Japanese people's inner transformation from the old value system of bushido into a new one, which would appreciate their individuality. Later on, Nitobe called the new application of bushido precepts plebeianism. In the end, the main theme of Nitobe's *Bushido* is not explaining the codes of bushido, but bridging the gap between bushido ethics and Christian ethics.

Bushido attracted public interests in Japanese people and culture at Japan's transitional period of achieving the status of a world power. It was a few years before Japan's involvement in the Russo-Japanese War from 1904 to 1905, followed by the Sino-Japanese War from 1894 to 1895. The credit for this great accomplishment belonged to Nitobe's drive for transmitting his ideas to the West, particularly to the U.S., in their language. Nitobe held a strong conviction that Japanese culture and American culture were respectively unique, and thus, Japanese people and American people could be on equal terms and understand each other. That is the premise of Nitobe's aspiration toward intercultural and intellectual cooperation between the two countries.

By publishing *Bushido*, Nitobe gained a foothold in his further pursuit of fostering cross-cultural understanding between Japan and the U.S., which will be examined in the following sections.

3. 日米交換教授としての働き

In the 1900s, anti-Japanese sentiment spread to many parts of the U.S., since people in Californian cities had agitated against Japanese immigrants, who had increased at the turn of the century. American workers thought Japanese workers to be a menace to their job opportunities, and local legislatures had already called for a Japanese Exclusion Act. Meanwhile, on the opposite shore in Japan, people were offended by the campaigns excluding Japanese immigrants from local communities in the West Coast states in America. This is when Nitobe was appointed as the first Japanese exchange professor and left for the U.S. The Carnegie Endowment for International Peace established the cultural and academic exchange program whose objective was to promote mutual understanding between the U.S. and Japan under those conditions.

Nitobe made his lecturing tour in the U.S., and visited the universities mentioned in Table 3 as well as other institutions, from September of 1911 to May of 1912. Six of those universities, Brown, Columbia, Johns Hopkins, Virginia, Illinois, and Minnesota, were involved in the exchange program. During his stay in the U.S., Nitobe made one hundred sixty-six lectures in English on Japan-U.S. relations and an outline of Japan and Japanese people, focusing on geography, history, religion, education, law, culture, and economy.

Table 3: Nitobe's Academic Lectures in the U.S. during the year 1911-1912

	Institution
1	Brown University
2	Columbia University
3	Johns Hopkins University
4	University of Virginia
5	University of Illinois
6	University of Minnesota
7	Stanford University
8	University of Chicago
9	Washington and Lee University

©2013 Maki Taniguchi

It is said that Nitobe's tour always drew big crowds, which reacted positively to his lecture. At Columbia University, John Dewy (1859-1952), who was teaching philosophy there, was in the audience, and listened to Nitobe with great interest. (Dewy visited Japan as an American exchange professor of the Carnegie program as well in 1919, and stayed at Nitobe's house in Tokyo.)

Nitobe's main addresses in the U.S. were compiled into *The Japanese Nation: Its Land, its People and its Life with Special Considerations to its Relations with the United States*. The publication (by G.P. Putnam's Sons) in 1912 was the fruits of Nitobe's efforts in America. A short time before Nitobe left the U.S., he wrote the preface. It conveys what Nitobe realized throughout lectureship in the following manner.

> To transmit a thought from one to another may not require an intellect of high order or an original cast of mind; but I am more than willing to play a second or even a third part, if I can thereby add a note—be it ever so low—toward the fuller harmony of diverse nations or of discordant notions. (*Nitobe Inazo Zenshu*. Vol.13, p.9.)

By using the metaphor of orchestral parts, Nitobe illustrated that his intention of developing cross-cultural understanding was to play the part of a mediator who acted as a link between two different cultures.

Finally, Nitobe found out the meaning of his long-cherished mission, to be a bridge across the Pacific Ocean. Nitobe's motivation for encouraging intercultural understanding was not merely introducing Japanese culture overseas. Nitobe regarded the mediator's role as an advocator of people's commonalities rather than differences. What Nitobe emphasized was that humans share a universal value, namely, human dignity. His experiences as an exchange professor led him to more a fundamental appreciation of international cooperation than before. He strove toward better understanding not only between Japan and the U.S. but also among other nations.

After coming back to Japan, Nitobe delivered lectures on the early history of the U.S. at Tokyo Imperial University in 1918, as part of a lecture series named after Alonzo Barton Hepburn (banker, 1846-1922). It was the first lecture course on American studies in Japan, and its purpose was to extend knowledge of the U.S. and its people. This time, Nitobe contributed to raising awareness of American culture in Japan and stressed the spirit of individuality underlying

American civilization. *Beikoku Kenkoku Shiyo* (An Outline of the Early History of the U.S.) in 1919 is a compilation of Nitobe's lectures for the Hepburn course.

Followed by his duty as Carnegie's exchange professor, Nitobe was assigned as the first Japanese Under-Secretary General of the League of Nations. Nitobe served from 1920 to 1926 in Geneva, Switzerland. As an advocator of human commonality and harmony, Nitobe was well qualified to undertake international service. One of the most outstanding achievements of Nitobe's tenure of office was his leadership for founding the International Committee on Intellectual Cooperation in 1922. This was an advisory board of the League of Nations and its aim was to advance international understanding through cultural and academic exchanges of scholars and artists. As you know, this agency laid the foundation of the United Nations Educational, Scientific and Cultural Organization (UNESCO), set up after World War II. Nitobe's assertion that all humans are one in the ultimate goal of building peace must have been inherited into the core values of UNESCO.

The first lecture tour in the U.S. built the groundwork for Nitobe's career development as an internationalist. In reality, Nitobe's contribution to the League of Nations was the peak of his lifework. After the Manchurian Incident in 1931, Japan-U.S. relations were on the brink of breaking down, and Nitobe struggled to reduce international tensions, as will be revealed in the next section.

4. 満州事変後の渡米

Nitobe's later years were full of trials, beginning with the Manchurian Incident on September 18, 1931. After the incident in China, Japan became increasingly isolated from international society. The world community severely condemned the militaristic policy of Japan. Under these conditions, Nitobe left for the U.S. again to explain Japan's position behind the incident.

From March of 1932 to April of 1933, without representing any organizations this time, Nitobe made a speech tour in the U.S. to rid American people of anti-Japan sentiment. It is a well-known fact that America was already one of the most influential powers in the world community. Nitobe intended to gain American people's recognition and to prevent Japan's isolation from international society. However, his voice was largely neglected by people in both Japan and the U.S., because they had their own interest in China and fears about their national security.

There is significant controversy over the pros and cons of Nitobe's peace-building activities in America after the Manchurian Incident. Some criticize him for justifying Japan's role in the incident, which was the very outset of the Japanese military's acts of violence throughout World War II. Others suggest that Nitobe envisioned a harmonious society, seeking reconciliation between nationalism and internationalism at that critical moment.

Both negative and positive effects of Nitobe's speech tour in America should be examined in order to fully understand his visions and actions in his later years. Unquestionably, Nitobe had little understanding of China or the background of the Manchurian Incident. Nitobe had faith that every person had an inner "seed", a potential to be civilized, irrespective of race or nationality. Based on this progressive view on civilization, which was grounded on his Quakerism, Nitobe tended to judge stages of civilization, and did not regard China as civilized enough to govern Manchuria. That is why Nitobe defended Japan's invasion of Manchuria. The downside of Nitobe's view needs to be kept in mind.

Nevertheless, at the same time, Nitobe's peaceful objectives must not be underestimated. When considering what brought Nitobe to America at the age of seventy, the following article entitled "Cheering Advice to a Traveller" (on May 1, 1932) gives a clue to recognizing his motive. Nitobe wrote this article for a series "Editorial Jottings" for the Japanese English dailies *Osaka Mainichi* and *Tokyo Nichi Nichi*.

> On the eve of my departure on a rather disagreeable journey, I called on the Okina to bid him farewell. In wishing me *bon voyage*, he said:—"About fifty years ago I was sent on a very trying mission. The country to which I was bound presented an appearance of utter darkness. I strained my eyes, as it were, to see some light to lead and comfort me. Failing to find any, my heart sank within me and I felt like giving up the mission. Then a Voice within me said—Go on, depending on the light that is within you! I felt greatly encouraged, because within me I harboured no thought of gain or ambition. I could say to myself that 'my strength was as the strength of ten because my heart was pure.'" (*Nitobe Inazo Zenshu*. Vol.16, p. 350.)

Okina is a fictitious character which Nitobe created for the "Jottings," and is said to be Nitobe's old acquaintance and mentor. If you pay attention to Okina's remarks, you will notice that Okina is Nitobe's persona. Nitobe stated his ideas and feelings by borrowing Okina's words.

In this way, the column indicates Nitobe's distressful choice. It implies that he summoned the courage to do what was right at that moment. He knew that this speech tour would be more painstaking than the tour as the exchange professor about twenty years earlier. (Nitobe misrepresented the professorship in the above.)

However, Nitobe was determined to carry out his original intention at any cost. He decided to follow his "inner light" and to work to bridge the gap between the public perceptions of the Manchurian Incident in the U.S. and Japan. After all, for Nitobe, it was following God. Nitobe practiced Quakerism and pursued his grave mission of furthering international cooperation to the end.

In this connection, Nitobe had to go back on his word in order to visit the

U.S. When the Immigration Act of 1924 finally took effect in America, Nitobe resented the unfair treatment of Japanese immigrants there, and he declared that he would not go to the U.S. until the act was revised. The law limited the number of immigrants through a quota system based on their origins. It also included a provision which prohibited those who were ineligible for naturalization from entering into the U.S. According to the then nationality laws, people from Asian countries were excluded from acquiring citizenship. As a result, in real terms, the immigration act did no longer allow Japanese people's entry into the U.S. Nitobe made such a declaration to show his opposition to this law and disappointment at American people's intolerant attitudes toward Japanese people. He was apprehensive that the enforcement of the act would deepen the split between Japan and the U.S.

After the Manchurian Incident, there came an urgent need for Nitobe to break his promise and leave for the U.S., instead of saving face by keeping it, as there were much more tensions between American people and Japanese people than there used to be. This decision implicitly suggests that Nitobe's trip to the U.S. was beyond self-interest.

As shown in Table 4, Nitobe was eager to meet with influential people in the U.S., such as local leaders and scholars of various organizations. The most influential figures Nitobe met were Herbert Clark Hoover (1874-1964), U.S. President, and Henry Lewis Stimson (1867-1950), U.S. Secretary of State. On June 1, 1932, Nitobe visited the White House and saw Hoover, and discussed the precarious situations in Japan after the Manchurian Incident. Nitobe also had a meeting with Stimson, and talked about the declining liberal powers in Japan.

Above all things, Nitobe earnestly delivered lectures at the invitations of universities, local institutions, Japanese associations, and academic societies. It should be emphasized that Nitobe focused more on promoting cultural and academic understanding at the individual level than the political or diplomatic level. That is the reason why Nitobe was lecturing in the U.S. as a private

Table 4: An Itinerary of Nitobe's Speech Tour in the U.S. during the Year 1932-1933

Dates (month/day/year)	Activities
4/14/1932	Leaves Yokohama
4/27/1932	Arrives at San Francisco
4/28-5/5/1932	Lectures around the area of San Francisco
5/6/1932	Arrives at New York
5/7/1932	Interviewed by the *New York Times* press
5/8/1932	Appears on the CBS radio, and gives a speech on "Japan and the League of Nations"
5/20/1932	Appears on the WOR radio, and gives a speech on "Japan's Hopes and Fears"
5/21-31/1932	Lectures around the area of New York
6/1/1932	Meets with Herbert Hoover and Henry Stimson at the White House
6/2-mid 6/1932	Lectures around the area of Washington, D.C., and meets with local leaders
mid 6-7/26/1932	Takes a rest in Philadelphia, receives an honorary degree from Haverford College, attends the graduation ceremony at Westtown School, and gives talks at Quaker meetings
7/27/1932	Lectures at the Williamstown Institute of Politics for 4 weeks (Speeches include a keynote speech "Development of International Coöperation" and "Basic Principles of Japanese Politics")
8/20/1932	Appears on the CBS radio, and gives a speech on "Japan and the Peace Pact"
late 8/1932	Meets with politicians in Ottawa, Canada, and is interviewed by the local press in Toronto
9/1932	Lectures at the Chicago Council on Foreign Relations
10/5/1932	Gives lectures, "Lectures on Japan", at University of California for two months
12/2/1932	Arrives at Riverside
12/11-16/1932	Lectures at the Tenth Institute of World Affairs (Speeches include "Japan's Place in the Family of Nations" and "Blending of the East and West in Japan"
late 12/1932	Takes a rest in California
early 1/1933	Lectures around the area of Oregon and Washington
1/13/1933	Lectures at University of Washington, and gives a speech to a Japanese association in Seattle

Dates (month/day/year)	Activities
1/17/1933	Gives a speech to the Washington State Legislature, in relation to a resolution carried by the legislature in appreciation of Nitobe's goodwill toward better U.S.-Japan relations
1/18/1933	Lectures at Teachers College, Bellingham, and leaves from Seattle to Vancouver, Canada
1/19-20/1933	Gives a speech to the Canadian Club, lectures at University of British Columbia, delivers talks to local Japanese organizations in Stevenson, and appears on a local radio
1/21/1933	Leaves from Vancouver, Canada to Los Angeles
2/12/1933	Gives speeches to Japanese American organizations in Southern California, and lectures at the Institute of International Affairs on "A Japanese Tribute to Abraham Lincoln"
3/1/1933	Receives an honorary degree from University of Southern California
3/6/1933	Leaves San Francisco
3/24/1933	Arrives at Yokohama

©2013 Maki Taniguchi

citizen. Again, Nitobe made more than one hundred speeches on Japanese culture and people in addition to speeches on the Manchurian question. Nitobe's manuscripts of the lecture series at University of California were put together for publication as *Lectures on Japan* in 1936.

Therefore, Nitobe's activities were not necessarily limited to defending Japan's position behind the Manchurian Incident. Rather, Nitobe's intention was to help people in the U.S. better understand the core qualities of Japanese culture and people. Nitobe's initiatives for peace were meant to cultivate any opportunity for a dialogue between Japanese and American people. As mentioned in the previous section, Nitobe firmly believed that peacebuilding would start with finding commonalties and respecting each other's standpoint through cultural and academic exchanges.

In conclusion, both the negative and positive aspects of Nitobe's trip to America were anchored in his own Quakerism, which was the guiding principle in his life. Still, one substantial question is how to evaluate those double-edged

Nitobe's activities in his later years. So, the final section will reassess the bridge-builder's work.

5. 日米の相互理解の架け橋

Nitobe came back home from his long lecturing tour in the U.S. on March 24, 1933. Only three days later, Japan formally withdrew from the League of Nations. The principles of the League of Nations had resonated with Nitobe, and he had been working for Japan's internationalization more than anyone. However, now, the whole situation was proceeding in the opposite direction—Japan's isolation from international society and the acceleration of militarism. How Nitobe felt about the course of events might be beyond all imagination.

However, Nitobe never stopped trying. He became even more eager to work for the development of Japan-U.S. relations. A few days after his return, Nitobe delivered a speech to the Tokyo Pan-Pacific Club. To the large audience, including American people, Nitobe stated that Japan was still a member of the family of nations, a natural institution, even though it left the League of Nations, an artificial institution. Nitobe reiterated Japan's place in the family of nations and its willingness to stay open to the world community. Notably, Nitobe articulated his idea about the relationship between Japan and the U.S. in the speech as follows:

> America is not a member of the League of Nations, but it is one of the greatest and at present perhaps the most powerful members of the family of nations, so our relations with that country must demand our deepest and most careful consideration. Therefore, though the clouds that hang over the Pacific at present are still quite dark, yet with an effort and a will to bring about better understanding, we shall, I hope,

regain our position in the heart of the American people. (*Nitobe Inazo Zenshu*. Vol.23, p. 378.)

Nitobe considered mending ties with the U.S. to be a priority matter in those serious times. Furthermore, Nitobe held that citizen diplomacy was a key to preventing Japanese people's anti-foreignism as well as to restoring American people's goodwill.

America represented Nitobe's ideal of the spirit of democracy, in other words, respect for each individual's dignity. In the process of Japan's modernization, Nitobe stressed that the notion of personality was what Japanese people needed to adopt above all things. Nitobe believed that the advancement of American civilization was not realized without this fundamental principle. That explains why Nitobe so admired the U.S. and its people and pursued his dream of becoming a bridge between Japan and America all his life.

In retrospect, Nitobe's labor for peacebuilding remained fruitless. Also, as discussed in the previous section, his questionable progressive view on civilization, which is inseparable from his own Quakerism, must not be overlooked. Still, one thing is certain—Nitobe aimed to promote dialogue between the conflicting viewpoints of Japanese and American people until the end of his life.

In 1933, Nitobe passed away from disease in Victoria, Canada, after attending the Pacific Conference in Banff. The conference was organized by the Institute of Pacific Relations, which was a non-governmental body for discussing issues of trans-Pacific countries in terms of scientific research. Nitobe became Japan's Chief Director to the institute in 1929. Since then, he participated in the institute's conference every other year as the leader of the Japanese delegation. He originally planned to embark upon another lecturing tour in the U.S. after the Banff conference. Although that was never accomplished, the scope of Nitobe's peacebuilding efforts is worthy of attention. Nitobe was always concerned about the relationship between Japan and the U.S., which were two of the major Pan Pacific countries. Regarding the ties between the two counties, Nitobe took a broad view. Nitobe's activities for fostering Japan-U.S relations spanned various levels, from the League of Nations on the official level to the Institute of Pacific Relations on the grassroots level.

It is remarkable that a non-native speaker had a command of English firm enough for extending mutual understanding between Japan and the U.S. As Table 5 suggests, about half of Nitobe's works, including scripts of speeches

Table 5: A List of Nitobe's Publication in English

Year	Title
1891	*The Intercourse between the United States and Japan*
1893	*The Imperial Agricultural College of Sapporo, Japan*
1900	*Bushido: The Soul of Japan*
1909	*Thoughts and Essays*
1910	*The Influence of the West upon Japan*
1912	*The Japanese Nation*
1914	"China's Chance for a Republic"
1920	"Japanese Colonization"
1920	*What the League of Nations Has Done and Is Doing*
1921	"Esperanto and the Language Question at the League of Nations"
1925	*The League of Nations Movement in Japan*
1929	"The Use and Study of Foreign Languages in Japan"
1929	*Two Exotic Currents in Japanese Civilization*
1929	*The Japanese Traits and Foreign Influences*
1931	*Japan: Some Phases of her Problems and Development*
1931	*Japan's Public Economy and Finance*
1934	*Reminiscences of Childhood in the Early Days of Modern Japan*
1936	*Lectures on Japan*
1938	*Editorial Jottings*
Others	2 articles to *Friends Review* (1885) 3 articles to *Interchange* (1886-87) 28 articles to *Osaka Mainichi* (1929-33) 2 articles to *Proceedings of the Institute of World Affairs* (1933)

©2013 Maki Taniguchi

and contributed articles, were written in English. This fact shows that Nitobe himself wisely matched his Japanese way of thinking with the Western way of thinking.

The footprints of Nitobe's journey show how rewarding and frustrating his endeavors as a bridge across the Pacific Ocean were. Whereas Nitobe's sense of values was enriched by his life experiences among different peoples, at the same time, it was afflicted by conflicting viewpoints among them. Ultimately, the bridge builder's task was to endure holding discordant viewpoints, connect them, and transform them into mutual understanding.

Nitobe set a high value on cultural and academic cooperation, as he believed that a better relationship between Japan and the U.S. could not be realized without a transformation of people's views and minds. Nitobe's approach toward peacebuilding in both countries in those crucial years is an indispensable asset for understanding America and America people from another angle.

執筆者紹介

藤村　敬次（ふじむら・けいじ）第1章
株式会社国際コミュニケーション研究所 代表取締役。自社にて社内英語公用語化を推進し，企業研修，ビジネス英語講座で活躍。主に製造業，サービス業にて，ESP（目的別英語）アプローチを用いたオリジナルテキスト執筆。また自身の運営する教室では個々のニーズにあったESPコースを展開。企業・大学（KDDI，京都大学，関西学院大学，等）にて英語学習法，グローバルキャリアについての講演多数。著書に『英字新聞日経ウイークリー活用法3』（大学教育出版，2012年，共著）がある。

立花　顕一郎（たちばな・けんいちろう）第2章
㈱日経国際ニュースセンター勤務を経て，現在は東北文化学園大学総合政策学部准教授。立教大学兼任講師。著書（共著）に，『英字新聞日経ウィークリー活用法』（大学教育出版，2010年），World News Report from VOA: Learn American English and Much More（Cengage Learning，2008年）等がある。

秋葉　丈志（あきば・たけし）第3章
1975年アメリカ・メリーランド州生まれ。国際教養大学准教授。2010年カリフォルニア大学バークレー校大学院修了（法社会学 Ph.D.）。アメリカと日本における憲政・憲法のあり方をそれぞれの歴史的・社会的文脈において捉える研究を進める。著書に『トマス・ジェファソンと議会法』（成文堂，2008年，共著），「裁判官たちのダイアローグ－国籍法違憲判決の文脈的分析―」『法社会学』第76号（2012年），「アメリカの人種マイノリティを巡る憲法論と社会実態」『法社会学』第77号（2013年）等がある。

山元　里美（やまもと・さとみ）第4章
1973年鹿児島県生まれ。水産大学校水産流通経営学科准教授。2008年イリノイ大学大学院アーバナ・シャンペーン校修了（社会学 Ph.D.）。主な研究領域は，アメリカの不法移民，労働運動，トランスナショナリズム/グローバリゼーション。著書に「エンパワメント支援に見られる「自己の力」と「他者の力」の交錯 ― シカゴ市のワーカーズセンターの事例解釈 ―」『移民研究年報』第19号（2013年），"Fair Price for Whom?: A Critique of Fairness and Justice in the Albany Park Workers' Rights Campaign" The Japanese Journal of American Studies 第22号，『英語で学ぶ現代アメリカ水産業』（大学教育出版，2011年）等がある。

西川　秀和（にしかわ・ひでかず）第5章
1977年大阪生まれ。専門は歴代アメリカ大統領。2009年，早稲田大学社会科学研究科博士後期課程修了。2005年，早稲田大学社会科学部助手。2007年，大阪外国語大学非常勤講師（大

阪大学外国語学部に改組を経て現在に至る)。著書に,『歴史が創られた瞬間のアメリカ大統領の英語』(ベレ出版, 2008 年),『冷戦レトリックの形成過程 ― トルーマン大統領のレトリック戦略を中心に』(早稲田大学出版部, 2009 年),『ジョージ・ワシントン伝記事典』(大学教育出版, 2012 年),『ジョン・アダムズ伝記事典』(大学教育出版, 2013 年),『アメリカ大統領制度史 上巻』(デザインエッグ, 2013 年),『アメリカ大統領制度史 下巻』(デザインエッグ, 2013 年) 等がある。

河内　信幸 (かわうち・のぶゆき) 第 6 章

1950 年愛知県生まれ。1973 年金沢大学法文学部卒。1981 年立教大学大学院文学研究科博士課程満期退学。博士 (文学) (金沢大学)。現在, 中部大学国際関係学部・同大学院国際人間学研究科教授。その間に, ハーヴァード大学客員研究員, オハイオ大学客員教授。アメリカ現代史・国際関係史専攻。主な研究領域は, 1930 年代のニューディールから戦後のアメリカ社会。編著書に『ニューディール体制論 ― 大恐慌下のアメリカ社会 ― 』(学術出版会, 2005 年),『グローバル・クライシス ― 世界化する社会的危機 ― 』(風媒社, 2011 年),『現代アメリカをみる眼 ― 社会と人間のグローバル・スコープ ― 』(丸善プラネット, 2012 年) 等がある。

大賀　哲 (おおが・とおる) 第 7 章

1975 年東京都生まれ。2005 年英国エセックス大学政治学部博士課程修了 (Ph.D. in Ideology and Discourse Analysis)。神戸大学大学院国際協力研究科・助教を経て, 2008 年より九州大学大学院法学研究院・准教授 (国際政治学・アジア政治論)。この間, オックスフォード大学セントアントニーズコレッジ・客員研究員, ケンブリッジ大学アジア中東学部・客員研究員など。主要業績として『東アジアにおける国家と市民社会 ― 地域主義の設計・協働・競合』(柏書房, 2013 年),『北東アジアの市民社会 ― 投企と紐帯』(国際書院, 2013 年, 編著),『国際社会の意義と限界 ― 理論・思想・歴史』(国際書院, 2008 年, 共編著) 等がある。

谷口　真紀 (たにぐち・まき) 第 8 章

1975 年山口県生まれ。2012 年関西学院大学大学院言語コミュニケーション文化研究科博士課程後期課程修了, 博士 (言語コミュニケーション文化)。現在, 同研究科研究員および滋賀県立大学非常勤講師。研究領域は, 新渡戸稲造の信仰と実践。論文に「新渡戸稲造のクエーカー信仰」『言語コミュニケーション文化』第 10 号 (2012 年 12 月),「晩年の新渡戸稲造とアメリカ ― 満州事変後のアメリカ講演をめぐる評価」『アメリカ研究』第 47 号 (2013 年 3 月) 等がある。

■編者紹介

杉田　米行（すぎた・よねゆき）

1962 年大阪府生まれ。
1999 年 5 月ウィスコンシン大学マディソン校博士課程修了、Ph.D.（アメリカ史）。
現在、大阪大学大学院言語文化研究科教授。
主な研究領域は外交・安全保障、日米医療保険史。
主要業績として、Peter N. Stearns ed., *Demilitarization in Contemporary World History*（University of Illinois Press, forthcoming 共著）、Caroline Rose and Victor Teo, eds., *The United States between China and Japan*（Cambridge Scholars Publishing, 2013 共著）等。

英語で知るアメリカ
― 8 つのテーマで超大国の実情に迫る ―

2013 年 10 月 30 日　初版第 1 刷発行

■編　　者――杉田米行
■発 行 者――佐藤　守
■発 行 所――株式会社 **大学教育出版**
　　　　　　〒700-0953　岡山市南区西市 855-4
　　　　　　電話(086)244-1268㈹　FAX(086)246-0294
■印刷製本――サンコー印刷㈱
■Ｄ Ｔ Ｐ――北村雅子

© Yoneyuki Sugita 2013, Printed in Japan
検印省略　　落丁・乱丁本はお取り替えいたします。
本書のコピー・スキャン・デジタル化等の無断複製は著作権法上での例外を除き禁じられています。本書を代行業者等の第三者に依頼してスキャンやデジタル化することは、たとえ個人や家庭内での利用でも著作権法違反です。

ISBN978-4-86429-231-3